INSIGHT ● GUIDES

PRAGUE
POCKET GUIDE

⊙ Walking Eye App

YOUR FREE EBOOK AVAILABLE THROUGH THE WALKING EYE APP

Your guide now includes a free eBook to your chosen destination, for the same great price as before. Simply download the Walking Eye App from the App Store or Google Play to access your free eBook.

HOW THE WALKING EYE APP WORKS

Through the Walking Eye App, you can purchase a range of eBooks and destination content. However, when you buy this book, you can download the corresponding eBook for free. Just see below in the grey panel where to find your free content and then scan the QR code at the bottom of this page.

Destinations: Download essential destination content featuring recommended sights and attractions, restaurants, hotels and an A–Z of practical information, all available for purchase.

Ships: Interested in ship reviews? Find independent reviews of river and ocean ships in this section, all available for purchase.

eBooks: You can download your free accompanying digital version of this guide here. You will also find a whole range of other eBooks, all available for purchase.

Free access to travel-related blog articles about different destinations, updated on a daily basis.

HOW THE EBOOKS WORK

The eBooks are provided in EPUB file format. Please note that you will need an eBook reader installed on your device to open the file. Many devices come with this as standard, but you may still need to install one manually from Google Play.

The eBook content is identical to the content in the printed guide.

HOW TO DOWNLOAD THE WALKING EYE APP

1. Download the Walking Eye App from the App Store or Google Play.
2. Open the app and select the scanning function from the main menu.
3. Scan the QR code on this page – you will then be asked a security question to verify ownership of the book.
4. Once this has been verified, you will see your eBook in the purchased ebook section, where you will be able to download it.

Other destination apps and eBooks are available for purchase separately or are free with the purchase of the Insight Guide book.

TOP 10 ATTRACTIONS

ASTRONOMICAL CLOCK
Its fascinating rituals celebrate the passing of time. See page 50.

WENCESLAS SQUARE
Dominated by the iconic statue of the saint. See page 63.

ST VITUS CATHEDRAL
Prepare to be dazzled by its awe-inspiring facade. See page 32.

STERNBERG PALACE
Houses a fine collection of European Masters. See page 29.

NATIONAL THEATRE
The home of the National Opera and Ballet. See page 65.

LORETO
Fine frescoes adorn one of Bohemia's most important centres of pilgrimage. See page 40.

JEWISH QUARTER
Monuments remember a vanished community. See page 55.

CHARLES BRIDGE
A Gothic masterpiece, lined with beautiful sculptures, atmospheric at any time of day. See page 47.

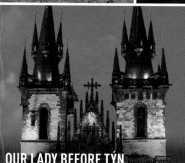

OUR LADY BEFORE TÝN
The church's Gothic spires soar into the sky. See page 52.

OLD ROYAL PALACE
The spectacular dimensions of Vladislav Hall seem out of this world. See page 36.

A PERFECT DAY

9.00am

Breakfast
If you have skipped breakfast at your hotel grab some coffee and something to eat at the charming Cukrkávalimonáda café (Lázeňská 7) in the Lesser Quarter.

12 noon

Nový Svět and lunch
Close to Hradčany Square is the delightful street of Nový Svět ('New World'). In one of the beautiful old houses is the restaurant U Zlaté Hrušky ('The Golden Pear'), a good place to try classic Czech cuisine.

2.00pm

Castle tour
After lunch head back to Hradčany Square and enter the castle gate. Spend the afternoon visiting St Vitus Cathedral, peeping into the beautifully-decorated Wenceslas Chapel, and the historic rooms of the Old Palace and the splendid medieval Vladislav Hall.

11.00am

Viewpoint
From Malostranské Square make your way up the steep street of Nerudova, lined with historic buildings, and climb up the steep ramp of Ke Hradu to Hradčany Square. From here there is a wonderful view across the city's domes and spires.

10.00am

St Nicholas
Just around the corner, on Malostranské Square, is the Church of St Nicholas, a Lesser Quarter landmark. This has one of the finest Baroque interiors in the city, glittering with gold leaf after renovation.

IN PRAGUE

5.00pm

Charles Bridge

Walk along Tomašská back to Malostranské Square where Mostecká will take you down to the Charles Bridge. Enjoy the late afternoon views along the river and of the castle hill. Back in the Lesser Quarter you can have a pre-dinner drink with more riverside views at Hergetova Cihelná (Cihelná 2b).

4.00pm

Formal gardens

After visiting the palace continue on through the castle to the formal Baroque gardens that cascade down the hill below Prague Castle. These are a delightful way of returning to the Lesser Quarter and they will bring you out onto Valdštejnské Square.

9.30pm

On the town

Experience the magic of the Old Town at night by crossing the illuminated Charles Bridge and continuing along Karlova to the Old Town Square. Round off the evening with a cocktail – along Pařížská you will find the Cloud 9 (Pobřežní 1), Bugsy's (Pařížská 10), Ocean Drive (V Kolkovně 7) and Tretter's (V Kolkovně 3).

7.00pm

Dinner options

When it comes to dinner there are a number of excellent options close by. The romantic Pálffy Palác (Valdštejnská 14) is lovely for a dinner for two, or if you are in search of good local dishes try either U Patrona (Dražického náměstí 4) or U Modré kachničky (Nebovidská 6).

CONTENTS

INTRODUCTION

Located in the heart of Europe – perhaps a little further north and west than most people think – Prague (*Praha* in Czech) is set on the banks of the Vltava River (a tributary of the Elbe). The site was chosen both for its strategic advantages and for its beauty, and the heart of the old city nestles in a bowl formed by rolling hills.

Some destinations still have the capacity to give even the most cynical tourist pause for thought, refusing to be reduced to a mere list of museums or galleries. Prague is one such. Never destroyed by war, the city's 1,000-year history is etched into its very fabric, its sublime beauty and unique character forged through its development as a major European Capital. It has been the capital of Bohemia for centuries. During the Middle Ages it rose to prominence as the capital of Charles IV (1316–78), the Holy Roman Emperor and ruler of much of Western Europe. In the late 16th and early 17th centuries the city was the seat of the Habsburg Court and it became the capital of the newly independent country of Czechoslovakia in 1918. The Communists took over in 1948 and ruled from the city, but they were overthrown in the Prague-based 'Velvet Revolution' of 1989. And when the Czechs and Slovaks parted company in 1992, Prague became capital of the new Czech Republic.

Prague always was and still remains a city of contrasts. It is famous for its illustrious artistic past and

'Five towns'

Prague used to be known as the 'five towns', after the five historic districts at its heart. These are: Hradčany (the Castle District), the Old Town (Staré Město), the Lesser Quarter (Malá Strana), the New Town (Nové Město) and Josefov (the Jewish Quarter).

present – in painting, sculpture, music, literature, architecture and design – yet is equally renowned for its beer, hearty food and sometimes boisterous tourist scene. Prague is also a city of protest and revolution, asserting its own identity, from the 15th-century Hussites who fought against the hegemony of the Catholic Church, to the struggle against Communist domination in 1968 and, more successfully, 1989. Yet, this is also a city that has gleefully embraced consumerism, seen in the flash new shopping malls that have sprung up. But these are all part of Prague's attraction; there probably is just about something for everyone, especially if you look just a bit beyond the standard tourist circuit of the Castle and Old Town Square.

Old Town Square

CITY OF ONE HUNDRED SPIRES

Prague's architectural tapestry spans almost every major European style, with fine examples of Romanesque, Gothic, Renaissance, Baroque, Art Nouveau and Modernist interwoven across the city. The facades show the work of master painters and sculptors, and behind them have worked some of the most famous of European musicians, including Mozart, Dvořák and Smetana. Also part of the fabric are the threads of political and religious intrigue.

Pride of place must go to Prague Castle, the seat of royal power throughout the Middle Ages. It sits on the top of a low ridge, casting a watchful eye over the city. Royal patronage spawned a court, which in turn drew the rich and powerful. These families spent fortunes building fine mansions and summer palaces using the finest craftsmen of their time. The Church also played its part, but the situation was complicated: Bohemia at this time represented a major battleground between partisans of Catholicism and church reformers. The many impressive cathedrals, churches, chapels, convents and monasteries erected here attest to the vehemence of the struggle – and the eventual triumph of the Catholic Church – and have given Prague the epithet 'city of one hundred spires'.

ART, CULTURE AND LEISURE

Centuries of the cream of music, theatre and art have nurtured a cultured and urbane society: the people of Prague appreciate their theatres and galleries as much as the visitors do, revelling in the artistic legacy of the Habsburg years and the flourish of artistic endeavours that accompanied the nationalism of the 19th century.

⊙ THE VLTAVA

As Prague's architecture envelops you in all its glory, you could be forgiven for overlooking one of the city's most beautiful sights: the Vltava itself, its graceful S-shape unwinding in the heart of the city. At times going under its German name of Moldau, for centuries it has inspired writers and musicians alike, notably Bedřiich Smetana whose symphonic poem dedicated to the river celebrates its lengthy journey across the Czech landscape on its way to Prague.

That said, people are just as at home in the city's numerous beer halls or going to a smoky jazz club or rock bar. The café society that nurtured many of the city's artists, from Kafka to Havel, is now largely a thing of the past and you are much more likely to see people enjoying an ice cream or driving around town in the ubiquitous Czech-produced Škoda cars than discussing philosophy.

Charles Bridge attracts many visitors

THE MODERN CITY

There have been many changes since 1989 for both the city and its people. The younger generation has grown up with the kinds of freedom long taken for granted by teenagers in the West and in many ways Prague is little different from any other large European city. Since the Velvet Revolution many historic buildings have benefitted from a massive renovation programme. However, not all of this has been sensitive or preserved the authenticity of the buildings. You will certainly find it difficult to avoid your fellow travellers, be they honeymooning couples, students on a budget European tour or large groups tramping en masse across the city squares. And yet Prague still remains one of Europe's most beautiful and fascinating places to explore. That it manages to satisfy the disparate demands of all these different groups is a testimony to the city's tenacity in clinging on to its treasures and their diversity.

A BRIEF HISTORY

More than most peoples, the Czechs are aware of the history that has moulded them and which continues to affect their present and influence their future. In its present form as an independent democratic republic, their country has existed only since 1992; before that, as a little nation, they were more often than not subjected to interference and domination by larger and more powerful neighbours.

BEGINNINGS

Located at a natural fording place on the Vltava River, a tributary of the Elbe River, Prague was settled as early as the Stone Age, and remains including tools and jewels have been found in the area. Celtic tribesmen settled here well over 2,000 years ago, followed by a Germanic people. Of more lasting significance, however, was the arrival in the 5th or 6th century AD of the first Slavs, ancestors of the Czechs, who chose to settle on the hilltops for safety. The second half of the 9th century saw the construction of the castle's original fortifications. It was from here that the Czechs were ruled by the Přemyslid family, a dynasty with mythical roots that extended well into the Middle Ages.

Přemyslid origins

Legend has it that Princess Libuša, leader of a Slavonic matriarchal tribe, picked the farmer Přemysl to be her husband. She told him to look for a village on the banks of the Vltava and to found a town there, which she said would achieve great things. This later became Prague, the 'golden city'.

A SAINTLY PIONEER

In the late 9th century the Greek missionaries Cyril

and Methodius brought Christianity to the Slavic lands. In around 873, Methodius baptised Prince Bořivoj and his wife Ludmila. Cyril and Methodius went on to be canonised, as did Ludmila, proclaimed patron saint of Bohemia following her assassination. The grandson of Ludmila, first of the rulers named Wenceslas (Václav in Czech), held the crown in the 10th century. During his reign a church

King Wenceslas

dedicated to St Vitus was built at Prague Castle. Wenceslas, who was a fervent believer, became the first of the Czech princes to be murdered while carrying out his holy duties. He was ambushed on his way to Mass and the killer turned out to be none other than his younger brother, Boleslav.

Far from being condemned for eliminating Wenceslas, Boleslav assumed power. During his reign, a well-travelled Jewish merchant by the name of Ibrahim ibn Jacob wrote admiringly of Prague as a great and busy trading centre with solid stone buildings. The town became a bishopric in 973, at about the time that the monastery of St George was established.

In the early 11th century Přemyslid rule was extended to neighbouring Moravia by Břetislav I, the great-grandson of Boleslav. He later became a vassal of the German emperor, paving the way for centuries of German influence. Břetislav's son, Vratislav II, was the first monarch to bear the title of King of Bohemia.

THE WENCESLAS DYNASTY

Prince Wenceslas I, the saint, was not the only Wenceslas I. The second Wenceslas I became king of Bohemia in 1230, and ruled long and well. Encouraging the arts, he presided over a growing prosperity – and population. However, the greatest of the Přemyslid rulers was Ottakar II (1230–78), known as the 'King of Gold and Iron' for his prowess in war and the prosperity he brought the kingdom. Ottakar encouraged German merchants, miners and craftsmen to settle in Bohemia and he founded the Lesser Quarter as a German enclave, protected by German law. His ambitions were terminated when he was slain in battle by his Austrian rival for the imperial throne, Rudolf of Habsburg, but under Wenceslas II, Otakar's son, the economy boomed thanks to large finds of silver, and the Prague groschen became a stable international currency.

The dynasty's luck eventually ran out with the son of Wenceslas II. In the summer of 1306, early in his reign, the teenage King Wenceslas III went down in history as the last of the Přemyslid kings when he was assassinated in Moravia.

CHARLES THE GREAT

The Přemyslid dynasty was succeeded by the House of Luxembourg. The first ruler was John (Jan) of Luxembourg, but it was his son Charles IV (Karel IV) who was to shine as ruler of the city. Ruling for 36 years, Charles was deeply involved in the government of Prague and Bohemia. His warm relations with the church led to Prague being promoted to an archbishopric in 1344. Under his direction, centuries of work began on the present St Vitus Cathedral. Early in his reign in 1348, Charles put Prague firmly on the intellectual map by founding Central Europe's first university. He expanded the city to the New Town, thus providing room for artists, craftsmen and merchants from all over Europe.

Finally, he gave Prague its Gothic Charles Bridge. In 1355, Charles acquired yet another royal title when he was crowned Holy Roman Emperor.

RELIGIOUS STRIFE

Prague should have thrived as the administrative headquarters of the empire that Charles had consolidated, but people and events conspired against it. Charles IV's son and successor, Wenceslas IV, proved an

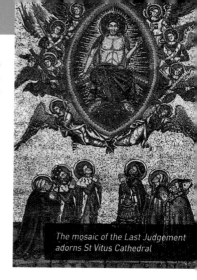

The mosaic of the Last Judgement adorns St Vitus Cathedral

irresolute leader. He turned his back on revolts and wars and was eventually deposed. In the biggest crisis that Wenceslas failed to address, Prague lived through the skirmishes that were preludes to the Reformation. At Bethlehem Chapel, in the Old Town, a theologian and professor named Jan Hus challenged the excesses of the Catholic Church. Hus's demands for reform became so vigorous that he was excommunicated, arrested for heresy and burnt at the stake in 1415. In the aftermath of his death his large and loyal following, known as the Hussite Movement, gained momentum, to the dismay of the papacy.

THE FIRST DEFENESTRATION

In 1419 a reformist mob invaded Prague's New Town Hall, liberated imprisoned Hussites and threw several Catholic city councillors from the windows. This event, called the First Defenestration of Prague, was to herald a long tradition. The harried brother of

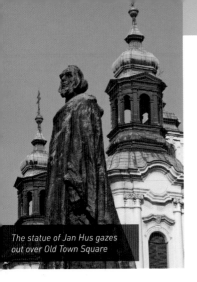

The statue of Jan Hus gazes out over Old Town Square

the unfortunate Wenceslas, Emperor Sigismund, marshalled Czech Catholic forces and foreign allies in a crusade against the Hussites. However, the rebels fought back. Their under-equipped, but highly motivated, peasant army won some noteworthy victories, such as at the Battle of Vítkov Hill. The rebels were commanded by a brilliant one-eyed soldier named Jan Žižka, but following his death the leadership foundered, and they were eventually defeated.

Sigismund died without leaving a successor. He was followed by the short-lived reigns of his son-in-law Albrecht of Austria, and then of Albrecht's son, Ladislas. A dynamic politician by the name of George of Poděbrady, who was implicated in the death of Ladislas, was elected to succeed him. George aligned himself with the Hussites, to the displeasure of the neighbouring Catholic kings and the papacy. He was eventually excommunicated and, along with Prague, boycotted by the international diplomatic and business community.

ARRIVAL OF THE HABSBURGS

Absentee kings ruled Bohemia from George's death until 1526, when the Habsburgs claimed the throne. This zealously Catholic dynasty held sway over what remained of the Holy Roman Empire and focused their attention on protecting their European borders against the very real Ottoman threat. By now the Protestant faith had become a powerful influence, in addition to which Bohemia's grave religious divisions were simply another thorn in their side.

In 1576 Emperor Rudolph II came to the throne and moved his capital from Vienna to Prague. Imperial patronage spurred the arts and sciences to new heights, and splendid Renaissance buildings further embellished the city. Rudolph's principal accomplishment was a decree granting freedom of religion to Catholics and Protestants alike. However, the decree was not honoured by Ferdinand II, the Catholic king who succeeded him in 1611, and the inherent religious conflict soon escalated.

The defenestration of 1618, was the starting signal for the disastrous Thirty Years War. A new king, Frederick of the Palatinate, was elected, but in 1620 his Protestant army was routed by the imperial forces on a low hill just outside Prague. What became known as the Battle of White Mountain has gone down as one of the blackest days in Czech history; its aftermath was marked by the public execution of leading Protestants and the expulsion from the country of all those who refused to convert to Catholicism.

Ferdinand's decisive victory radically changed the now-haggard face of Prague. The period that followed was characterised by later historians as the 'Darkness', a time when Czechs were a suppressed majority in their own land, their elite either dead or in exile, their language downgraded, and their favoured religion forbidden. Much of this was true. Confiscated Protestant estates were sold at knockdown prices to Habsburg

Uncanny pursuits

Rudolph II (1583–1611), Prague's emperor under the Renaissance, was fascinated by the occult. He employed a number of alchemists who had access to the castle by means of a network of underground passages.

supporters, many of them of foreign, particularly German, origin. German became the language of polite society, and Czech was eventually spoken only by peasants and the urban poor. Jesuits and other religious orders strove to eliminate the last sparks of Protestantism. However, not all was gloom. Once the country had recovered from the decades of war, a building boom beautified cities and countryside with the glories of Baroque art and architecture. However, the tensions arising between Prague's German-speaking and Czech-speaking citizens would persist well into the 20th century and have unforetold repercussions.

NATIONAL AWAKENING

In the 18th century Habsburg rule became more enlightened, notably in the reign of Emperor Joseph II (1780–90). His educational reforms produced a generation of literate Czechs, who

⊙ THE SECOND DEFENESTRATION OF PRAGUE

Cornered in Prague Castle by their angry Protestant adversaries on 23 May 1618, two terrified imperial officials begged for mercy, but their pleas went unheeded. Bundled to the window along with their unfortunate secretary, they were forced out, though one of them clung desperately to the sill until his knuckles were broken by a sharp blow from a dagger. Their descent into the moat far below should have killed them, but to everyone's surprise, they survived the fall, and succeeded in making their escape. According to the Catholic version of the event, they were miraculously borne up by the Virgin Mary; the possibly more realistic Protestant account describes how their fall was broken by the monstrous mound of rubbish that had accumulated in the moat.

became increasingly aware of their past history and their present subjugation. In the early 19th century a new intellectual elite emerged, codifying the Czech language, reviving its literature and agitating for Czech rights within the Empire. By the end of the century, Prague, which Emperor Franz Josef had described earlier as looking 'every bit a German city', was completely in the hands of the Czechs; street signs

Prague's National Theatre, symbol of Czech national pride

in German had disappeared, and bombastic buildings like the National Museum and National Theatre expressed an ever more confident Czech nationalism.

THE 20TH CENTURY

When the heir to the Habsburg throne, Archduke Franz Ferdinand, was assassinated in June 1914, the Austro-Hungarian Empire was plunged into World War I. From the ashes of a defeated Austria-Hungary, an independent Czechoslovak republic was proclaimed in October 1918, comprising Bohemia, Moravia and Slovakia. The first president of the First Republic was Tomáš G. Masaryk, an admired professor of philosophy.

WORLD WAR II AND AFTER

However, simmering tensions between the Czech and Slovak majoity and the country's sizable German minority

The Prague Spring was brutally crushed by Soviet tanks

came to a head when, in 1938, Hitler demanded self-determination for Czechoslovakia's German-speaking citizens. In order to appease him, Britain and France handed over the country's borderlands. In March 1939, after persuading Slovak nationalists to secede and form an ostensibly independent, near-Fascist 'Slovak State', Hitler incorporated the remainder of the country into Greater Germany as the 'Protectorate of Bohemia-Moravia'. Six long years of brutal occupation were to follow before Soviet troops liberated the city in May 1945.

At the parliamentary elections of 1946, the communists won nearly 40 percent of the votes. The non-communist pre-war president Edvard Beneš, elected again, invited the veteran communist leader Klement Gottwald to form a coalition cabinet. When, in 1948, several non-communist ministers resigned in protest at his policies, Gottwald packed the government with supporters. When the very popular non-communist Foreign Minister Jan Masaryk, son of Tomáš, was found dead below his office window at the foreign ministry it was whispered that he was the victim of another defenestration.

Gottwald, as the new president, framed a five-year economic plan, cracked down on the churches and purged his opponents outside and inside the party; scores were executed and thousands arrested. The show trials went on under Antonín Novotný, while farmers were forced into collectives.

The short-lived 'Prague Spring' of 1968 saw an attempt by reform Communists led by the Slovak Alexander Dubček to transform the system and create a 'Socialism with a human face'. This failed, crushed by the Soviet tanks which overran the country in August. For the next two decades, reinstated hardline Communists ruled the roost, buying off the populace by filling the shop shelves with consumer goods, albeit of poor quality. The few dissidents, among them playwright Václav Havel, suffered routine harassment and persecution.

THE CZECH REPUBLIC

In November 1989 the so-called Velvet Revolution saw Václav Havel elected as president, an office he was to hold for 13 years. While successive governments struggled with the problems of converting the Communist system into a free-market economy, Havel fought for the survival of the country whose freedom he had suffered for. In vain: in 1992, the Czech prime minister Václav Klaus and nationalist Slovak leader Vladimir Mečiar decided

⊘ THE VELVET REVOLUTION

On 17 November 1989, an event took place that should have been a peaceful student demonstration turned into a mass movement after police attempted to quell the event by clubbing protesters. Thousands then gathered on Wenceslas Square to call for the introduction of democracy, rattling their house keys as a symbol of protest against 40 years of communism. The next day, the regime stepped down in what would become known as Eastern Europe's quietest revolution.

Former president Václav Havel

that the only way to settle their differences was for Czechoslovakia to be divided. Avoiding the referendum that would almost certainly have put paid to their plans, they engineered the 'Velvet Divorce', the creation of separate Czech and Slovak Republics. The disappointed Havel submitted himself to re-election as president of his now diminished country, finally being replaced by Klaus in 2003. Despite setbacks, the Czech Republic has steadily integrated itself into the political and economic systems of the West. Membership of NATO came in 1999, and in 2004 the country joined the European Union. A flood in 2002 devastated towns and villages along the Vltava, including Prague.

While recent years have seen Prague prosper, since 2006 the country has experienced a high degree of political instability, with no one party able to command a majority in parliament. In 2013 a corruption and abuse-of-power scandal led to the fall of PM Petr Necas followed by early elections. The political situation did not stabilise until January 2014 when Bohuslav Sobotka became the head of the new coalition government. Sobotka attempted to dismiss the government amidst a scandal involving his finance minister and coalition partner, the billionaire Andrej Babiš, over his tax arrangements, but, amidst protests, the government completed the term. In October 2017, Babiš's centrist populist ANO 2011 party won nearly 30 percent of the vote.

collection of **Baroque Art in Bohemia** (Hradčanské náměstí 2; www.ngprague.cz; Tue–Sun 10am–6pm), which features works by two of the most important Czech painters of the era, Petr Brandl (1668–1735) and Jan Kupecký (1667–1740). Next to it stands the Salm Palace (details as above) which houses the National Gallery's collection of **19th-century Art from Neo-Classicism to Romanticism**, including

The National Gallery of European Art at the Sternberg Palace

landscapes by Josef Navrátil (1798–1865), August Piepenhagen (1791–1868) and Antonín Mánes (1784–1843).

The most ornate building on the square is the **Archbishop's Palace** (Arcibiskupský palác) sitting just next to the castle entrance. The house became the Archbishop's Palace after the Counter-Reformation in 1562 and its position was an indication of the power of the Catholic Church and its influence on the Habsburg monarchy. The facade was redesigned in the 1760s in rococo style.

Next door to the palace is another of the major art galleries of Prague. A cobbled alleyway leads to **Sternberg Palace ❸** (Šternberský palác, Hradčanské náměstí 15; www.ngprague.cz; Tue–Sun 10am–6pm), home of Franz Sternberg who was a great patron of the arts during the late 18th century. The handsome Baroque building now houses the Czech Republic's **National Gallery of European Art** (Národní galerie). Its fine body of old masters dating from the 14th to the 18th century serves as a reminder that the Habsburg dynasty was the most powerful of its time, ruling over its vast empire, in which Prague was one of the leading cities. Their collection incorporates work by the finest artists of their respective eras. Flemish and Dutch art features particularly strongly with works by the Brueghel dynasty, along with Peter Paul Rubens, Rembrandt and Frans Hals. Italian artists are represented by a wealth of 14th- and 15th-century decorative pieces from churches in Tuscany. Among the later paintings, works by Tintoretto and El Greco stand out. Perhaps the most noted painting in the collection is to be found in the Austrian and German section. Along with works by Hans Holbein and his son hangs the *Feast of the Rose Garlands* by Albrecht Dürer, with two Habsburg family members depicted on the canvas.

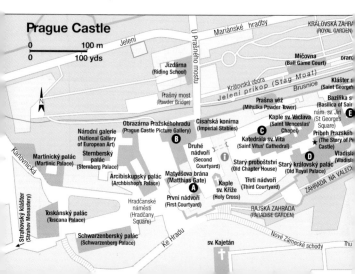

Prague Castle

0 — 100 m
0 — 100 yds

Jeleni
Mariánské hradby
KRÁLOVSKÁ ZAHRA (ROYAL GARDEN)

U Prašného mostu

Jízdárna (Riding School)

Míčovna (Ball Game Court)
oran.

Královská obora (Stag Moat)
Jelení příkop
Brusnice

Klášter s (Saint George

Prašný most (Powder Bridge)

Prašná věž (Mihulka Powder Tower)

Bazilika s (Basilica of Sai nám. sv. Jiri (St George's Square) **E**

Obrazárna Pražskéhohradu (Prague Castle Picture Gallery) **B**

Cisařská konírna (Imperial Stables)

Kaple sv. Václava (Saint Wenceslas' Chapel) **C**

Příběh Pražskéh (The Story of P Castle)

Národní galerie (National Gallery of European Art)

Sternberský palác (Sternberg Palace)

Druhé nádvoří (Second Courtyard)

Katedrála sv. Víta (Saint Vitus' Cathedral)

Martinický palác (Martinic Palace)

Arcibiskupský palác (Archbishop's Palace)

Starý proboštství (Old Chapter House)

Starý královský palác (Old Royal Palace) **D**

Vladisla (Vladisla

Matyášova brána (Matthias Gate) **A**

Kaple sv. Kříže (Holy Cross)

Třetí nádvoří (Third Courtyard)

ZAHRADA NA VALECH

Kanovnická

Strahovský klášter (Strahov Monastery)

Hradčanské náměstí (Hradčany Square)

První nádvoří (First Courtyard)

RAJSKÁ ZAHRADA (PARADISE GARDEN)

Toskánský palác (Toscana Palace)

Schwarzenberský palác (Schwarzenberg Palace)

Ke Hradu

sv. Kajetán

Nové zámecké schody
Thu

PRAGUE CASTLE

Building work on the **Castle** ❹ (Pražský hrad; www.hrad.cz) was begun in the 9th century. By the beginning of the 14th century it housed the royal palace, churches and a monastery. Refurbished during the reign of Charles IV, it was ravaged by fire in 1541 and most of the buildings were reconstructed in Renaissance style. The castle eventually became a backwater when the Habsburgs chose Vienna as their permanent base, but in the mid-18th century it was given its present unified appearance by Empress Maria Theresa and her Italian architect Nicola Pacassi. After Czechoslovak independence in 1918, it became the seat of the country's president, and was thoroughly renovated by the Slovene architect Josep Plečnik. Surrounding the walls are many gardens offering a peaceful retreat from the sometimes crowded rooms and galleries within.

Enter the castle proper through the ornate gates crowned with heroic statues of fighting giants. Sombre, uniformed guardsmen maintain a

A benign spectre

Legend has it that the ghost of a large black dog haunts the Hradčanské náměstí entrance to Prague Castle. Between 11pm and midnight it appears, and far from being aggressive, it accompanies passers-by as far as the Loreto before vanishing into thin air.

Map labels:
Belvedér (Belvedere Palace)
Daliborka (Dalibor Tower) ⓗ
Bílá věž (White Tower)
Zlatá ulička (Golden Lane)
Černá věž (Black Tower)
Na Opyši
ⓕ
Jiřská
Lobkovický palác (Lobkowicz Palace)
Staré zám.schody
Chotkova
(GARDEN OF THE RAMPARTS)
PALÁCOVÉ ZAHRADY (PALACE GARDENS)
U Zlaté studně
Ledeburský palác
Valdštejnská
Valdštejnské náměstí
Valdštejnský palác (Wallenstein Palace)
Tomášská
Sněmovní
VALDŠTEJNSKÁ ZAHRADA
Sněmovna
Letenská

silent watch as you pass through. From this first courtyard – added in the 18th century – the **Matthias Gate** (Matyášova brána), the entranceway dating from 1614 that once formed a triumphal arch over moats (now filled in) leads to the second courtyard. Immediately ahead is the entrance to the **Holy Cross Chapel** (kaple svatého Kříže), built by Anselmo Lurago in 1753, which houses a display of the cathedral's numerous national treasures and the remains of some of the country's most revered individuals (Apr–Oct daily 10am–6pm, Nov–Mar 10am–5pm).

Housed on the north side of this courtyard, in what were once the castle stables, is the **Picture Gallery of Prague Castle** Ⓑ (Obrazárna Pražského hradu; www.hrad.cz; daily Apr–Oct 9am–5pm, Nov–Mar 9am–4pm). The gallery displays works mainly collected by Rudolf II during his reign (1583–1612). Much of the collection of this passionate man of the arts was taken to Vienna in the years after his reign or lost to the Swedish forces who took it as booty in 1648. Still, the gallery boasts some superb works by Tintoretto, Veronese and Rubens. Here visitors can also enter the north gardens through an archway.

St Vitus Cathedral

A narrow passage leads to the third courtyard of the castle and a sudden view of the immense facade of **St

Fabulous mosaic

Of particular note over the triple-arched arcade of the Golden Portal is the mosaic of the Last Judgement, created by Venetian artists in 1370. It is composed of glass, pieces of quartz and other natural stones, as well as sheets of gold leaf slipped between two stones for a gilded effect. The Virgin Mary, John the Baptist, the Apostles, Charles IV and his wife Elizabeth of Pomerania are all represented, not forgetting the six patron saints of Bohemia.

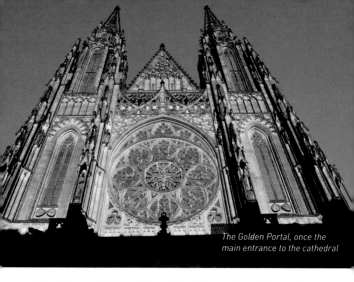

The Golden Portal, once the main entrance to the cathedral

Vitus Cathedral (katedrála svatého Víta; www.katedralasvateho vita.cz; Apr–Oct Mon–Sat 9am–5pm, Sun noon–5pm, Nov–Mar Mon–Sat 9am–4pm, Sun noon–4pm; charge), looming up just a few steps away. The towers and spires dwarf the surrounding buildings, at first glance altering one's perception of scale.

The first church on this hallowed ground was built in the 10th century by Prince Wenceslas, who was interred in the rotunda after his premature death. The present edifice was begun in 1344 on the occasion of Prague being declared an archbishopric. Charles IV decided that the new cathedral should be in the style of the great religious buildings of France and invited Matthew of Arras to design and build it. After Matthew's death, the work was continued by Peter Parler, a German architect, then by his two sons. Work was disrupted during the Hussite uprisings and was intermittent through the following centuries, in fact the whole building was not regarded as complete until 1929. The main entrance is now through the west doorway, but until the 19th century it was the south door – or Golden Portal – that provided entry. The porch of the latter doorway is highly decorated and crowned with an ornate mosaic of the *Last Judgement*. To the left, a Gothic window is filled with gold filigree work.

Once visitors have entered the cathedral, its gigantic proportions are immediately apparent. There are over 18 separate chapels lining the walls. The 19th- and 20th-century elements of the cathedral (near the main entrance) contain a chapel with stained glass by Alfons Mucha, greatly admired for his Art Nouveau artwork. However, the eye is automatically drawn down the core of the building to the magnificent chancel built by Parler in the 1370s. The towering vaults, decorated with delicate tracery, are a high point in Gothic architectural achievement. These are underpinned by elaborate stained-glass windows.

Several of the chapels in this area of the cathedral deserve further examination but none more so than **Wenceslas Chapel** (kaple svatého Václava), dedicated to Saint Wenceslas or the Good King Wenceslas of the Christmas carol as he is more commonly known. Parler created a wonderful Gothic room to house the tomb of the prince, on the

Stained-glass window by Alfons Mucha in the cathedral

same spot as it had been in the previous Romanesque rotunda. The walls are decorated with precious stones and gold leaf interspersed with several ornate frescoes illustrating scenes from the life of the saint. Above the chapel is a small room containing the coronation jewels. Seven separate keys are needed to unlock the door to the chamber and the jewels remain out of view except for on certain state occasions.

The silver tomb of John of Nepomuk

Next to the Wenceslas Chapel are stairs leading to the **crypt** where you can see the walls of earlier religious structures. This room holds the remains of Charles IV and members of his family, along with the tomb of Rudolf II. Above the crypt, in the main level of the cathedral, several other noteworthy rulers are interred: Ferdinand I lies in a large white marble tomb with his wife, and son Maximilian; and an ornate silver tomb holds the remains of Jan of Nepomuk, who was thrown from Charles Bridge in 1393 and declared a saint in the early days of the Counter-Reformation.

To the north of the cathedral you will find the **Mihulka Powder Tower** (Prašná věž), part of the 15th-century defensive walls and later used as a foundry and gunpowder workshop. During the reign of Rupert II rumours abounded that experiments in alchemy were being conducted here. It now contains an exhibition dedicated to the history of castle guards.

Vladislav Hall

The Royal Palace

The third courtyard of the castle opens out to the south of the cathedral. Walk past the old chapterhouse where you will find a heroic statue of St George. On the east side of the courtyard is the entrance to the **Old Royal Palace ⓓ** (Starý královský palác; www.hrad.cz; daily Apr–Oct 9am–5pm, Nov–March 9am–4pm), home to Bohemian rulers from the 11th century till the Habsburg takeover. Its somewhat modest facade conceals a fascinating building whose architectural style spans several centuries. The Romanesque early palace forms the foundations of the present structure, built during the last years of Přemyslid rule. Charles IV later enlarged the palace but it was Vladislav Jagiello in the late 1400s who created the opulent throne chamber. When it was completed in 1502, **Vladislav Hall** (Vladislavský sál) was the largest unsupported secular hall in the world and today its wide expanse and roof supported by ribbed vaults is one of Prague's highlights.

In the 17th century the hall was used as a meeting place, but in earlier times royal tournaments were held there with competitions in horsemanship. The horses were ridden up a wide, gently sloping staircase to the hall, which is now used by the many groups who tour the palace. Serious business went on in the two rooms leading off Vladislav Hall. The **Bohemian Chancellery** (Česká kancelář) was used for Bohemian government business, and it was from this room that the two imperial councillors and their clerk were defenestrated in 1618, precipitating the Thirty Years' War. The **Diet Hall** (Stará sněmovna) was the medieval parliament room. It was badly damaged in the fire of 1541 and rebuilt in the style of the time.

The Old Royal Palace also houses the **Story of Prague Castle** exhibition, which uses castle models, films and artefacts in an innovative way to tell the long and fascinating history of Prague Castle.

St George's Basilica

From the Royal Palace, walk east to another open square: St George's (náměstí U svatého Jiří). On the corner is the deep-red Baroque facade of **St George's Basilica E** (Bazilika svatého Jiří; daily Apr–Oct 9am–5pm, Nov–Mar 9am–4pm), founded in the early 9th century and said to be the oldest surviving church in Prague. The interior is austere in true Romanesque style, although it has been extensively restored over the centuries, with the scant remains of original ceiling frescos. The basilica is the resting place of Queen Ludmila, patron saint of Bohemia, and other members of the Přemyslid dynasty.

At the end of the 9th century **St George's Convent** (klášter svatého Jiří) was established next to the basilica. The religious sanctuary was rebuilt many times over the centuries before finally being dissolved in 1782.

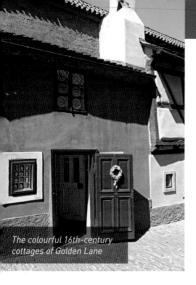
The colourful 16th-century cottages of Golden Lane

The Eastern Sector of the Castle

From the convent it is only a short walk to the eastern sector of the castle. **Golden Lane F** (Zlatá ulička; daily Apr–Oct 9am–5pm, Nov–Mar 9am–4pm; entrance fee also covers Dalibor Tower) nestles against the northern ramparts of the castle, lined with a wonderful array of old cottages dating from the 16th century. They were first occupied by archers conscripted to defend the castle and later by craftsmen, goldsmiths included, to whom the street owes its name. Some said that the street was even a dwelling place for alchemists. By the beginning of the 20th century, it was an enclave for the poor. The writer Franz Kafka lived here in 1916 with his sister. Today the cottages have been restored and are home to souvenir shops. Just watch your head as you enter, as the lintels are extremely low.

Three attractions fill the route from Golden Lane to the east gate. **Lobkowicz Palace G** (Lobkovický palác; www.lobkowicz events.cz; daily 10am–6pm), built in the aftermath of the 1541 fire, houses many of the star items from the outstanding collections of the princely Lobkowicz family. Among them are paintings by Canaletto and Velázquez as well as *Haymaking* by Pieter Brueghel, the pride of the National Gallery before its restitution to its original owners. There are also original scores by Mozart and Beethoven, as well as a large display of armour.

MALÁ STRANA

Lying below the castle and stretching to the banks of the Vtlava River is **Malá Strana**, the Lesser Quarter or Little Quarter. The area was first settled in the 13th century when Otakar II invited German craftsmen to settle in Prague. Several fierce fires destroyed the early town, so although the street plan remains faithful to Otakar's original instructions, the majority

Strahov's Philosophical Library

of the buildings date from a later period. Following the Counter-Reformation in the mid-17th century, Malá Strana became fashionable with courtiers and aristocrats, and their money was invested in mansions replete with Renaissance and Baroque details. This is still a residential area, a factor which gives it an intimate atmosphere tangibly different to that of Staré Město just across the river (see page 49).

LESSER QUARTER SQUARE

The heart of this quarter is **Lesser Quarter Square** (Malostranské náměstí) but its fine mansions, the arcades of which straddle the cobblestones, have been somewhat overshadowed by the busy tram stop here. In the centre of the square sits the **Church of St Nicholas ⑦** (kostel svatého Mikuláše; www.stnicholas.cz; daily Mar–Oct 9am–5pm, Nov–Feb 9am–4pm; concerts Wed–Mon Apr–Oct 6pm), one of the most prominent buildings on the

Prague skyline and one of the architectural highlights of the city. The building is perhaps the crowning glory of the Dientzenhofer dynasty. Work began in the first years of the 18th century but the church was not finished until 1755. The distinctive 75-metre (245ft) dome dominates the surrounding buildings. The now renovated interior of the church is a Baroque masterpiece, with ceiling frescoes by the Viennese artist Johann Lukas Kracker featuring scenes from the life of St Nicholas, and Franz Palko's *Celebration of the Holy Trinity* gracing the inside of the dome. The two statues below that of St Nicholas above the altar are of St Ignatius Loyola and St Francis Xavier. The church organ has 2,500 pipes and 44 registers, and was once played by Mozart.

To the north of the square is the street of Letenská where you will see the **Church of St Thomas** (kostel svatého Tomáše; www.augustiniani.cz/en) abutting the road. Originally founded in 1257, it was one church that remained Catholic throughout the Hussite uprising, and at the onset of the Counter-Revolution became a major focus of Catholic worship. In 1723 the church was badly damaged during a storm, and Kilian Ignaz Dientzenhofer was commissioned to oversee its rebuilding. St Thomas was once the church of a large monastery that had the sole right to brew beer within Prague; the brewery closed in 1951, but the cellar is now home to the atmospheric St Thomas Brewery Bar (www.augustinehotel.com).

As you walk towards Malostranská metro station you pass the high walls of **Wallenstein Palace** (Valdštejnský palác; www.senat.cz; June–Sept Sat–Sun 10am–6pm, Apr, May and Oct until 5pm, Nov–Mar 10am–4pm on the first weekend of the month). Now the home of the Czech Senate, this extensive complex was the first Baroque palace in Prague and was built for Albrecht von Wallenstein, a favourite military commander of Ferdinand II. He began work on the palace in 1624 but soon fell victim to his own publicity: he was killed on the king's orders in 1634 when he was discovered to be holding secret talks with the enemy. The **gardens** (Apr, May, and Oct Mon–Fri 7.30am–6pm, Sat–Sun 10am–6pm; June–Sept until 7pm) feature a superb loggia, clipped hedges, fountains and statuary: copies of works by the celebrated sculptor Adriaen de Vries – the originals having been stolen by Swedish forces during the Thirty Years' War.

West of Lesser Quarter Square is **Nerudova**, named after writer Jan Neruda, who once lived here. There are a number of fine buildings on this street, each distinguished by an emblem as they were built before the introduction of street numbers. Look out for 'The Three Fiddles' at No. 12 or 'The Green Lobster' at No. 43. Thun-Hohenstein Palace at No. 20, its ornate entranceway framed by huge eagles, is now the Italian Embassy; the Morzin Palace at No. 5 now serves as a diplomatic base for Romania.

South of Lesser Quarter Square, the houses are a little less grand but the streets are peaceful and devoid of tourist shops. Walk down Karmelitská to find the **Church of Our Lady of Victories** (kostel Panny Marie Vítězná; www.pragjesu.info; museum open Mon–Sat 9.30am–5.30pm, Sun 1–6pm; free) on your right, named in honour of the victory at the Battle of White Mountain in 1620. Most visitors come

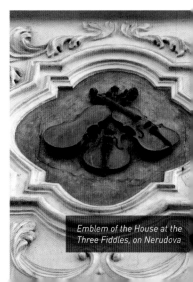

Emblem of the House at the Three Fiddles, on Nerudova

Boat on the canal at Kampa Island

to see the Holy Infant of Prague – a wax effigy brought from Spain in 1628 and said to work miracles.

From the church, cross the street and head east to **Maltese Square** (Maltézské náměstí), filled with Baroque palaces, many of which are now embassy buildings. The square is named after the knights of Malta who were granted the nearby 12th-century **Church of Our Lady Beneath the Chain** (kostel Panny Marie pod řetězem; www.maltezskyrad.cz; sightseeing by appointment only or before the mass) as a gift from King Vladislav. Here they built a large priory that provided protection for the Judith Bridge across the Vltava. The church's odd name refers to the chain used to close the monastery gates. Just round the corner at Saská 3 lies the **Karel Zelman Museum** Muzeum Karla Zemana; www.muzeumkarlazemana.cz; daily 10am–7pm) where you can explore the fantastical world of this famous Czech film director and animator through interactive exhibits.

KAMPA ISLAND AND PETFIÍN HILL

Located nearby, Grand Priory Square (Velkopřevorské náměstí) leads across a bridge to **Kampa Island** ❽. Here you will find a fading mural of John Lennon – a focus for youth unrest in the final days of Communist rule. The narrow branch of the river separating Kampa Island from the Lesser Quarter was once used to power watermills. Most of the island is now parkland, though at its northern end is na Kampû, a delightful cobbled square. A large mill on the banks of the Vltava has been imaginatively converted into the **Museum Kampa** (www.museum kampa.cz; daily 10am–6pm), with collections of 20th-century and contemporary art.

Go down Karmelitská and, as it becomes Újezd, you will see the green parkland of **Petřín Hill** ❾. The vast, open area stretching all across the hillside is in fact four different parks. Footpaths wind up to the summit, but it is far less taxing to take the **funicular** (www.dpp.cz) running constantly throughout the day and evening. Once at the top you can stroll along to explore the park's attractions. These include the **Observation Tower** – a mini Eiffel Tower built for the Prague Industrial Exhibition in 1891, a mirror maze, two chapels and a church, and the remnants of the **Hunger Wall** (Hladová zed') – a city wall built by Charles IV and said to have been a community project to provide work, and therefore food, for the poor. Not far from the Hunger Wall, on Ujezd, is the stark **Monument to the Victims of Communism**, unveiled in 2002.

CHARLES BRIDGE

East of Lesser Quarter Square is Mostecká (Bridge Street). This short, shop-lined road leads to the river and one of the highlights of a visit to Prague: **Charles Bridge** ❿ (Karlův most).

This 520-metre (1,700ft) -long bridge, one of the most famous in the world, was built across the Vltava in the mid-14th century following the destruction of the previous Judith Bridge in a flood. Charles IV and his architect, Peter Parler, were determined to build a bridge that would endure. But even they could not have imagined that it would last 600 years and counting. The original bridge was a very functional structure with little embellishment. At the Malá Strana end there were two towers: the **Judith Tower** (dated *c*.1190), the smaller of the two, survives as the only reminder of the Judith Bridge. The Lesser Quarter Bridge Tower was built as a gateway to the town. At the Old Town end of the bridge is the **Old Town Bridge Tower**, a masterpiece of Gothic architecture. Both towers are open to the public and offer splendid views of the city.

The numerous statues that now make the bridge unmistakeable were mainly added in the early 18th century when the Italian fashion for bridge decoration spread throughout Europe. The exception to this is the statue of **St John Nepomuk**, which was erected in 1683 on what was thought to be the 300th anniversary of his violent demise at the hands of King Wenceslas IV.

When his lifeless body was thrown from the bridge onlookers claimed that a holy spirit was seen rising from it, and the story heightened his revered status. The bronze relief below Nepomuk's statue, the one with five stars on the halo around the head, depicts the final moment of the saint; it is polished each day by the hands of thousands of tourists who hope it brings good luck.

The bridge carried traffic until the 1950s – until the mid-19th century it was

The Charles Bridge

the only way to cross the river – but is now reserved for pedestrians. During the day Charles Bridge can be one of the busiest parts of the city, as groups march determinedly between stops on the tourist trail. Numerous licensed artists set up stalls along its path to tempt you with water-colours or moody black-and-white photographs. More information on this city landmark can be found in the **Charles Bridge**

The relief depicting the demise of St John Nepomuk

Museum (Museum Karlova Mostu; Křižovnické náměstí 3; www. charlesbridgemuseum.com; daily 10am–6pm).

STARÉ MĚSTO (OLD TOWN)

While political power was invested in Hradčany, the **Old Town** (Staré Město) – a cluster of streets on the opposite bank of the river – was the commercial heart of Prague. The city sat on important trading routes, east–west from Krakow into Germany and north–south from Vienna to Warsaw. As the Bohemian *groschen* became one of the major currencies in Europe, so the city began to take on a grander appearance. Today it offers streets of architectural delights from the medi-eval to the Baroque. Old Town Square, at the heart of the Old Town and once the main marketplace for the city, is a good place to embark on a visit.

The Astronomical Clock

OLD TOWN SQUARE

Often considered to be the very centre of Prague, **Old Town Square** ⓫ (Staro-městské náměstí) is a focus for tour groups, carriage rides, bars, cafés and shopping. It is also one of the architectural highlights of the city. Of a large, irregular shape that has changed over the centuries, it has been dominated in modern times by a powerful **Monument to Jan Hus** (pomník Jana Husa), unveiled in 1915 on the 500th anniversary of the martyr's death. The **Old Town Hall** ⓬ (Staroměstská radnice; www.staro mestskaradnicepraha.cz; Mon 11am–6pm, Tue–Sun 9am–6pm) sits on the southwest corner of the square. A curious amalgamation of buildings in different architectural styles – its earliest elements date from the 14th century – it expanded as Prague grew in importance. Badly damaged in World War II, the north wing has never been rebuilt.

Although many interesting features adorn the exterior of the building, most visitors crowd to see the **Astronomical Clock** which was added in 1490. At the time, it was so highly prized by the city fathers that they had the clockmaker who made it blinded so that he could not re-create his masterpiece. On every hour, the figures on the clock perform their ritual. Death consults his watch and pulls a cord that rings a bell; Christ and the apostles appear above; and the crowing of a cock signals the end of the proceedings. The clock captures time in a variety of ways, from the passing seconds to the cycles of the sun and moon. It is interesting to note that, in keeping with the thinking of the time, the clock shows the earth positioned at the centre of the universe.

You can visit the inside of the Old Town Hall to see the council chambers with their superb tapestries and the recently renovated Oriel Chapel. Climb the Old Town Hall Tower, erected in 1364, for an excellent view of the surrounding streets and rooftops. Abutting the Old Town Hall is **Dům U Minuty**. With its distinctive *sgraffito* decoration it is one of the most memorable Renaissance buildings in Prague.

The west flank of the square altered dramatically in the late 20th century. A large, open area behind the Old Town Hall was cleared following the devastation wreaked during the last days of the German occupation. It now has benches where weary tourists can take a rest. The ornate facade of the **Church of St Nicholas** (kostel svatého Mikuláše; www.svmikulas.cz; Mon–Sat 10am–4pm, Sun noon–4pm) was once hidden down

⊘ EXECUTION SQUARE

Old Town Square used to serve as a backdrop to public gatherings and also executions. In 1437, 56 Hussite soldiers mounted the scaffold. On 21 June 1621, the 27 leaders of the uprising of 1618 were executed on the order of King Ferdinand II. Their number was made up of noblemen and ordinary citizens, Germans and Czechs alike. Twenty-four of the condemned were put to death by the same executioner. The event is commemorated by a plaque set in the wall of the Old Town Hall along with crosses planted in the ground.

Church of Our Lady before Týn

a narrow side street but today it appears as part of the north flank. Although a church has occupied this site since the 12th century, the present building dates from 1735. During World War I it served as the church of the Prague garrison, and at the end of the conflict was handed over to the constituted Czechoslovak Church. It is sometimes used to stage concerts.

The east flank is dominated by two buildings. The eye-catching rococo facade belongs to **Kinský Palace** (palác Kinských), designed by Kilian Deintzenhofer and built from 1755–65 by Anselmo Lurago. In 1948, from the palace balcony, Klement Gottwald made a speech that was instrumental in the communist takeover of the government. The palace houses the National Gallery's collections of **the Art of Asia** and **the Art of the Ancient World** (www.ngprague.cz; Tue–Sun 10am–6pm).

In stark contrast is the **Church of Our Lady before Týn** (kostel Panny Marie před Týnem; www.tyn.cz; Mar–Dec Tue–Sat 10am–1pm and 3–5pm, Sun 10am–noon), an immense Gothic edifice whose 15th-century towers rise to 80 metres (260ft) above the surrounding medieval streets. The church was a hotbed of heresy from its earliest days and became the main Hussite place of worship as the reform movement grew in popularity during the 16th century. Following the

Counter-Reformation, it was handed back to the Catholic Church and has remained steadfast to the present day.

AROUND OLD TOWN SQUARE

The streets surrounding Old Town Square are a delight to explore. Almost every building throws up some highlight, ranging from the tiniest detail – a doorknocker or carved lintel – to the grand statement, for example the superb Renaissance door of the **House at the Two Bears** (Dům u Dvou Zlatých Medvědů), on Melantrichova. There's no better way to explore this part of town than on foot, and much of the Old Town is pedestrianised.

West of Old Town Square, the area extending to the river is probably the most densely packed with fine mansions. However, it also has one of the highest concentrations of tourist shops. Next to Old Town Square is the much smaller **Malé náměstí**, decorated with a filigree fountain. On the west side of the square, it is the facade of Rott House (U Rotta; www.hotelrott.cz) that steals the show. It's decorated with paintings by acclaimed 19th-century Czech artist Mikoláš Aleš.

Karlova or **Charles Street** is the most direct route to Charles Bridge. Look out for the **Clam-Gallas Palace** (Clam-Gallasův palác), a magnificent Baroque building set with gargantuan statues by Matthias Bernard Braun. Just before you reach the river you will pass the high walls of the **Clementinum** (Klementinum; www.klementinum.com; daily guided tours every half an hour from 10am, Jan–Feb 10am–4.30pm, Mar–Oct 10am–6pm, Nov–Dec 10am–5.30pm, last tour one hour before closing), a former Jesuit college and the largest complex of buildings on this side of the river. The site was originally the Dominican monastery of St Clement, but was offered to the Jesuit brotherhood by Ferdinand I in 1556 to promote Catholic education. Work commenced on the Church of the Holy Saviour in 1593, and its domes now describe one of the most recognisable outlines in the city. By the middle of the 17th century the Jesuits had a monopoly on education in the city as the Hussite faculty of the Carolinum (see page 62) was disbanded. The Clementinum expanded as the university grew, resulting in a large part of the Old Town being demolished in 1653, although this process was not completed until one hundred years later. When the Jesuit brotherhood was dissolved by papal decree in 1773, the Clementinum became home to the library of the secular Charles University. Today it is the **National Library**, and its churches are used as venues for concerts. Also on the site is the fascinating Astronomical Tower, from which there are wonderful views over the Old Town.

The approach to Charles Bridge is marked by the small Knights of the Cross Square (Křižovnické náměstí), watched over by a majestic statue of Charles IV erected here in 1848 to mark the 500th anniversary of the founding of Charles University. On the north side is the **Church of the Knights of the Cross** dedicated to St Francis Seraphicus (svatého Františka Serafinského). The one church is solely open for services.

South of the bridge is the Novotného lávka, a jetty lined with buildings. Furthest away, with a wonderful view of the river, bridge and castle is the **Smetana Museum** (muzeum Bedřicha Smetany; www.nm.cz; Wed–Mon 10am–5pm), which pays homage to one of the country's most beloved composers and musicians.

South of Karlova is **Bethlehem Square** (Betlémské náměstí) where you will find a reproduction of the 14th-century **Bethlehem Chapel** (Betlémská kaple; www.bethlehemchapel. eu; daily 10am–6pm). It was here that Jan Hus embarked on his campaign to reform the Catholic Church, which ended in his execution. One main form of protest consisted in conducting Mass in Czech instead of Latin. Just around the corner from here is the

Rotunda of the Holy Cross, one of the three remaining Romanesque round churches in Prague.

THE JEWISH QUARTER

The area north of Old Town Square has quite a different character from the rest of the district. This is **Josefov**, once the base of one of the most active and influential Jewish communities in Eastern Europe and still home to an Orthodox community. To

French-style Pařížská

reach Josefov, walk down **Pařížská** ⑮, by the side of the Church of St Nicholas. This street, as the name suggests, is reminiscent of a leafy Paris boulevard complete with fine boutiques.

The Jewish community was founded in the latter years of the 11th century. Throughout the centuries the Jews were alternatively accepted and ostracised by the ruling dynasties. Certainly they were never allowed to expand beyond this small quarter. Despite a devastating fire in 1689 and the demolition of many buildings in the quarter in the 1890s to make way for new, more sanitary, housing, several important buildings remain. In the days leading to the genocide of the Jews by the Nazis in World War II, the treasures of numerous synagogues in Bohemia were brought to Prague for safekeeping and in order that a museum might be founded to document an extinct race. The collection is managed by the **Jewish Museum** (www.jewishmuseum.cz; Apr–Oct Sun–Fri 9am–6pm, Nov–Mar

Sun–Fri 9am–4.30pm), which oversees several museums housed in the synagogues of Josefov.

The **Old-New Synagogue** ⑯ (Staronová synagóga; not part of the Jewish Museum; www.synagogue.cz; Sun–Thu 9am–6pm, winter till 5pm only, Fri 9.30am–5pm) is the oldest surviving synagogue in Europe. Built at the beginning of the 13th century, it was named the New Synagogue but renamed Old- New when a newer synagogue, now demolished, was built nearby. It is one of the finest medieval buildings in the city. The main hall is reached through a small, arched doorway featuring an elaborate carving of a vine; the 12 bunches of grapes depict the 12 tribes of Israel. The interior walls bear traces of 13th-century frescoes and later inscriptions of sections of the Psalms. The brick gables on the exterior were added in the 15th century.

⊙ THE GOLEM

The giant man of clay called the Golem is Prague's equivalent of the Frankenstein monster. He is supposed to have been fashioned out of mud from the riverside by learned Rabbi Loew (c.1520–1609), master of many an arcane mystery. Obedient at first, the Golem performs his allotted tasks, but runs amok when the rabbi forgets to renew the charm that keeps him under control. Eventually he is overcome, and a spell reduces him once more to mud. His remains are shovelled up and stored among the rafters in the attic of the Old-New Synagogue, where they have been ever since. Woe betide anyone who has the temerity to disturb them! The most enduring image of the Golem is the one in the film of the same name, a silent-screen classic of the early cinema by the German director Paul Wegener.

Next to the synagogue is the **Jewish Town Hall** (Židovská radnice), the seat of the Chief Rabbi. Its pink, Baroque facade is crowned by a fine tower and two clocks, which tell the time in Hebrew and Roman numerals.

The entrance to a complex of two synagogues and the Jewish Cemetery lies on Široká. The ticket office here offers a special rate for one or all of the Jewish Museum attrac-

The Old Jewish Cemetery

tions; alternatively, you can buy tickets at each separate venue. At this site, the **Pinkas Synagogue** (Pinkasova synagóga; www. jewishmuseum.cz; tours only) began life as a private family place of worship, although it was later expanded to rival the Old-New Synagogue. Following the end of World War II, the names of all the Czech victims of the Holocaust were inscribed on the walls of this synagogue in a stark and powerful tribute to those who lost their lives.

Make your way through the outer courtyard of the Synagogue to reach the **Old Jewish Cemetery** (Starý židovský hřbitov; www. synagogue.cz; Sun–Thu 11am–5pm, winter until 4pm, Fri 10am–2pm; free). This small area was once the only burial ground for Jews and as such each plot was used by several generations of the same family. It is thought that over 12,000 gravestones have been placed here, the earliest surviving ones dating from 1429 and the most recent from 1787. The jumble of carved stones sits

The Spanish Synagogue

under the shade of mature trees. The **Ceremonial Hall** next to the cemetery was built in 1911 for the Prague Burial Society and now has an exhibition on Jewish life and traditions.

The **Klausen Synagogue** (Klausová synagóga) sits on the far side of the cemetery and was built on the ruins of a school, or *klausen*, in 1694. It displays artefacts relating to Jewish history and customs, including biographical information about the major figures of the Jewish community of Prague such as Rabbi Löw, who was suspected of working with the supernatural. His ornate tomb in the cemetery is regularly visited by well-wishers who have come to pay their respects. The Jewish Museum is responsible for two other synagogues. Nearby, **Maisel Synagogue** (Maiselova synagóga), on Maiselova, also began life as a private house of prayer – that of Mordachai Maisel who acted as banker to Emperor Rudolf II. The original structure was lost in the fire of 1689, but replaced by this ornate building, and it makes a fine backdrop to the collection of treasures it displays. Rare items of religious significance dating back to the Renaissance, including liturgical silver, textiles and manuscripts, can be viewed here.

Finally, a comparatively recent addition to the Jewish Museum is perhaps its pièce de résistance. The **Spanish Synagogue** ❼ (Spanělská synagóga; www.jewishmuseum.

cz), a little way east on Vězeňská, has been renovated and its 1860s Moorish architectural style and wall decoration are truly dazzling. The richness of the interior is in total contrast with the simplicity of the Old-New Synagogue. Displays recount the recent history of the Czech Jewish community.

ON THE BANKS OF THE VLTAVA

On the Outskirts of the Josefov are three attractions that are in no way associated with the Jewish community. The beautifully laid out **Museum of Decorative Arts** (Uměleckoprůmyslové muzeum; www.upm.cz) occupies a French-style neoclassical building whose rear overlooks the Old Jewish Cemetery. It is a showcase for all types of decorative art, at which the inhabitants of Bohemia have consistently excelled. The museum holds one of the world's largest collections of antique glass. There are also displays relating to ceramics, tapestries, costumes and clocks.

In the direction of the river stands the impressive, neo-Renaissance facade of the **Rudolfinum** (Dům umělců; www.ceskafilharmonie.cz), one of the finest concert venues in the city and home to the Czech Philharmonic Orchestra. It served as the seat of the Czechoslovak parliament immediately after independence in 1918.

Also on the banks of the Vltava, but a little way north, is **St Agnes's Convent** ⑱ (klášter svaté Anežsky). The convent was founded in the first half of the 13th century by the Poor Clares, and at its prime was a large complex of several churches and cloisters before falling into decay. Today the remaining buildings have been restored to house the National Gallery's outstanding collection of **Medieval Art in Bohemia and Central Europe: 1200–1550** (www.ngprague.cz; Tue–Sun 10am–6pm), including works by Master Theodoric, Lucas Cranach the Elder and Albrecht Dürer. The convent also acts as a venue for concerts and temporary exhibitions.

EAST OF OLD TOWN SQUARE

Beyond the Church of Our Lady before Týn, you will find a collection of narrow lanes which hold the pretty **Church of St James** (kostel svatého Jakuba), and a wide thoroughfare, **Celetná**. Now free of traffic, it was once the major entry route to the city from the east. A stroll along Celetná reveals fine houses, little alleyways, courtyards and deep cellars. Faint traces of Renaissance Prague are discernible among the Baroque decoration. The **House of the Black Madonna** ⑲ (dům U černé Matky boží) at No. 34 dates from the early 20th century. The huge windows of this Cubist masterpiece, built by Josef Gočár in 1911–12, reveal its original use as a department store. The statue after which the house is named is located in a niche set on the corner of the facade. Renovated in 1994, the building was home to the National Gallery's Museum of Czech Cubism until 2012, when

---

⊙ THE ROYAL ROUTE

The Powder Tower marked the start of the so-called Royal Route, the route which the coronation processions of the Bohemian kings and queens took through the city, and which linked Royal Court Palace and Hradãany Castle across the river.

Carriages would travel down Celetná, through Old Town Square and along Karlova, before heading across Charles Bridge. Once in Malá Strana they would travel along Mostecká into Lesser Quarter Square before making their way via Nerudova to St Vitus Cathedral in the castle compound. There, the new monarch would be crowned.

part of the collection was moved to Veletržní Palace (see page 72).

At the eastern end of the street is the **Powder Tower** 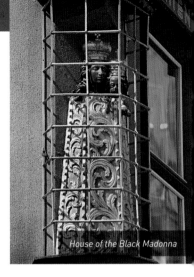 (Prašná brána; www.muzeumprahy.cz/prasna-brana; daily Apr–Sept 10am–10pm, Mar and Oct 10am–8pm, Nov–Feb 10am–6pm), a tower dating from the end of the 13th century. It was one of the gates into the Old Town and marked a transition from the previously

House of the Black Madonna

favoured defensive structure to a ceremonial entranceway. Originally, it was linked to a palace, called the Royal Court, which was demolished at the beginning of the 20th century after lying derelict for a number of decades. In its place – in the manner of a phoenix rising from its ashes – is one of Prague's foremost Art Nouveau buildings, the **Municipal House** (Obecní dům; www.obecnidum.cz; daily tours available). The complex was built in the first decade of the 20th century to provide an exhibition space as well as a modern auditorium located at the heart of the building. **Smetana Hall** is well established as one of the major arts venues in the city, and has a sumptuous café, a glittering French restaurant, and a huge Pilsner beer cellar.

From the Powder Tower, come back into the Old Town and one street south of Celetná is Železná, also pedestrianised. Halfway down the street you will see the wrought-iron adornment of the **Estates Theatre** (Stavovské divadlo; www.

narodni-divadlo.cz) ahead. Built in the 1780s, in its lines are some of the finest examples of neoclassical architecture in the city. Here on 29 October 1878, Mozart conducted the premiere of his new opera *Don Giovanni* in front of a rapturous audience. The theatre was also used as a set for the film *Amadeus*, directed by Czech Miloš Forman.

Next to the theatre lie the remains of the first university of Prague. The **Carolinum** (Karolinum) was founded by Charles IV and named after him. Jan Hus held the post of rector here and the campus became a hotbed of Hussite activity. After the victory of the Counter-Reformation it was handed over to the Catholic Jesuits and merged with their Clementinum complex near the river. Much of what remains here dates from the 18th century, but look for the beautiful oriel window overhanging the street between the Carolinum and Estates Theatre.

NOVÉ MĚSTO (THE NEW TOWN)

Charles IV gave the go-ahead for the building of the New Town (Nové Město) in 1348 when overcrowding in the Old Town was becoming an acute problem. Although much of the first stage of building has been swept away in subsequent redevelopment, the New Town has many important attractions. It is also a focus for hotels, and entertainment in the form of theatres, nightclubs and cinemas.

Na příkopě is the street that was the traditional dividing line between the Old Town and the New Town. It was built over the old moat, the defensive structure around the Old Town and links to the Powder Gate at its eastern end. Today it is pedestrianised, and is one of Prague's most important retail streets, lined with modern shops, restaurants, casinos and exchange offices.

WENCESLAS SQUARE

The southern end of Na příkopě meets **Wenceslas Square** ㉑ (Václavské náměstí), the symbolic heart of modern Prague for both independent Czechoslovakia and the Czech Republic. The scale of the square is truly impressive: more of a boulevard than a plaza, at first glance it brings to mind the Champs-Elysées in Paris. Huge crowds have gathered here, most notably in

St Wenceslas Monument with the National Museum

1968 to protest against the arrival of Russian troops, and in 1989 to cheer the fall of communism. Largely closed to traffic, the square is a popular place for a stroll.

Pride of place still goes to the **Café Evropa**, an Art Nouveau gem. The hotel to which it belongs was once the toast of the city and currently is closed for renovation. Also look out for the Wiehl House with its neo-Renaissance decoration by Mikoláš Aleš on the corner of Vodičkova.

At the top of the square sits the **St Wenceslas Monument**, crowned by a statue of the saint astride a noble steed. Below the great man are life-size statues of the other patron saints of Bohemia. The work of Josef Myslbek was erected in 1912.

Behind the monument is the **National Museum** ㉒ (Národní muzeum; www.nm.cz; daily 10am–6pm). Created at a time of rising national consciousness in the late 1880s, its neo-Renaissance styling makes a confident statement with a beautifully decorated

Fresco in the Church of Our Lady of the Snows

exterior and grand interior. The museum contains rather dull collections relating to mineralogy, archaeology and anthropology. Both buildings of the museum, at Václavské náměstí and at Vinohradská 1 are closed for reconstruction until 2018.

North of the museum along busy Wilsonova is the neoclassical **State Opera** (Státní opera; www.narodni-divadlo.cz). Beyond this is the main railway station built in Art Nouveau style. Just north of the square on Panská 7 is the small **Mucha Museum** (www.mucha.cz; daily 10am–6pm), dedicated to the Art Nouveau works of Alphonse Mucha (1860–1939); there's also a very good gift shop attached.

The bulk of the New Town lies to the southwest of Wenceslas Square, between the busy Sokolská and the river. Starting at the northwest end of Wenceslas Square and heading towards the Vltava you will come to **Jungmannova**. This is now one of the prime shopping areas of the city.

On the east side of Jungmann Square (Jungmannovo náměstí) is the **Church of Our Lady of the Snows ㉓** (kostel Panny Marie Sněžné; www.pms.ofm.cz; daily except times of masses); look out for a curious Cubist lamppost outside the northwest entrance. Founded by Charles IV to mark his coronation in 1347, this great Gothic church was intended to have three aisles, but work was interrupted by the Hussite uprising. What remains today is the chancel of the original plan, standing on its own and consequently looking completely out of scale in relation to its floor area.

THE NATIONAL THEATRE AND VICINITY

Follow Národni in the direction of the river to find the **National Theatre** ㉔ (Národní divadlo; www.narodni-divadlo.cz) and the New National Theatre. The former, an impressive building that adds grace to the riverfront vista, was built in the middle of the 19th century as the result of a passionate demand for an independent Czech theatre. In 1881, just before the theatre was due to open, it was completely destroyed by an accidental fire. However, such was the level of national pride at the time that within weeks the

The National Theatre

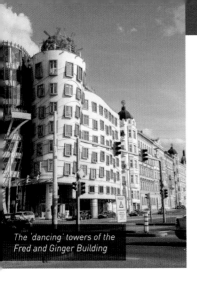
The 'dancing' towers of the Fred and Ginger Building

money had been raised to rebuild it, and it reopened in 1883 with a performance of Smetana's *Libuše*. Many of the finest Czech artists of their day were commissioned to work on the theatre, which was renovated in the 1980s when Karel Prager was commissioned to design the New National Theatre so as to expand the complex. This is one of the most striking examples of Communist-era architecture in the city, presenting three cubic buildings with facades of glass brick, and acts as a permanent home to the National Theatre Company and Lanterna Magika.

ARCHITECTURE OLD AND NEW

Next to the river you will see the **Slovanský ostrov** island to your left. The island did not exist until the early 18th century, but, following work to shore up its banks, it became the centre of social life in the city. Here, an ancient water tower is linked to the Manés Gallery, an edifice in the Bauhaus style that is one of the best examples of functionalism in Prague. The headquarters of the Manés group of artists who take their name from the 19th-century artistic dynasty, it has a changing programme of avant-garde exhibitions.

Further south down Masarykovo nábřeží (Masaryk riverside boulevard), on the corner of Resslova, is another example of modern architecture. The **Tančící dům** (www. tancici-dum.cz), or dancing building, by the architect Frank Gehry, has become known locally as the Fred and Ginger Building. A glass-and-concrete tower (Ginger) gives the impression of being held by the upright tower (Fred), as if caught in action on the dance floor.

Walk up Resslova to find the **Church of St Cyril and St Methodius** ㉕ (kostel svatého Cyrila a Metoděje; Sat 8–9.30am, Sun 9am–noon). Methodius, regarded as the father of Czech Christianity, was ably accompanied by St Cyril in his mission to preach the gospel. Built in the Baroque period (c.1730), this church was originally dedicated to St Charles Borromeo and served retired priests. It closed in 1783 but in the 1930s was reopened under the

⊙ MEMORIES OF THE RESISTANCE

On 18 June 1942, the Church of St Cyril and St Methodius became the scene of an unequal battle between the assassins of Reinhard Heydrich, the Nazi governor of Bohemia and Moravia, and German troops. The Czechoslovak parachutists sent from Britain to carry out the assassination threw a bomb at Heydrich's open-top car, then later sought refuge in the crypt. Unfortunately they had been betrayed. The whole area was sealed off and the crypt attacked by a battalion of the SS. The seven parachutists fought back determinedly for several hours, but their fate was sealed when the fire brigade was brought in to flood their hiding place. Not a single one of them was taken prisoner – they either perished in the fighting or took their own lives rather than surrender.

The New Town Hall

auspices of the Czecho-slovak Orthodox Church, hence the change of name. The church became embroiled in one of the tragic episodes of World War II when, after they had assassinated the brutal Nazi gover-nor Reinhard Heydrich, his killers were given sanctuary in the crypt. The Nazis exacted hor-rific revenge by ordering the village of Lidice to be burnt to the ground, the men shot, and the women and some of the children deported to concentration camps. A small memorial can be found outside the church where bullet holes from the incident are still visible. The crypt has been turned into a memorial museum (www.vhu.cz; Tue–Sun Mar–Oct 10am–5pm, Nov–Feb Tue–Sat10am–5pm) with photographs, docu-ments and memorabilia of the event.

The east end of Resslova meets **Charles Square** (Karlovo náměstí), the largest in the city. Laid out in the original city plan of 1348, it used to be the biggest market in Prague known as the Cattle Market. In the mid-19th century the square was transformed with the creation of a garden area, which today offers a place to relax. The surround-ing apartment blocks are not particularly exciting but the **Faust House** 26 (Faustův dům) has been preserved and refurbished. The history of the house, which was given its baroque appearance in the 18th century, stretches back to the 14th century, when it belonged to Prince Václav of Opava, an alchemist and natural historian. In the 16th century, it was home to Englishman Edward Kelley, charged by Emperor Rudolf II with turning base metal into gold. The many secretive practices carried out here fostered its association with the legend of Faust.

Walking north towards the Old Town you will find the **New Town Hall** ㉗ (Novoměstská radnice; www.nrpraha.cz) at the end of Charles Square. Building work started in 1348, and in 1419 it was the site of the First Defenestration of Prague (see page 17). Several additions were made in the 16th and 18th centuries, but it is the 15th-century tower that is still the building's crowning glory. Before strolling back into the main part of the town, take a detour to **U Fleků** on Křemencová (www.ufleku.cz). Now a tourist trap, this beer hall has been open since 1499. It only serves the strong dark beer brewed on its premises.

Close to the I.P. Pavlova metro station is the Baroque **Vila Amerika**, completed in 1720. Designed by Kilián Ignáz Dienzenhofer, it was originally used by the Michna family as a summer palace. Today it houses the **Dvořák Museum** ㉘ (muzeum Antonína Dvořáka; www.nm.cz; Tue–Sun 10am–1.30pm and 2–5pm), with memorabilia relating to one of the greatest Czech composers. There are recitals during the summer, although recorded compositions by Dvořák are played when the musicians are not present.

Prolific composer

Dvořák composed an impressive number of works in his lifetime: 31 pieces of chamber music, 50 orchestra scores and nine symphonies, including the famous Slavonic Dances.

Around the corner, at No. 12–14 Na bojišti, is the **Chalice Restaurant** (U Kalicha; www.ukalicha.cz), famous for being the favourite drinking hall of Jaroslav Hašek, author of *The Good Soldier Svejk*.

OUTLYING AREAS

Some of the suburbs of Prague have a preponderance of dour modern apartment blocks to house the growing population. However, not all are so grim and there are a number of attractions that make a trip out on the metro or tram well worth the effort.

VYŠEHRAD

Vyšehrad (Vyšehrad metro station; www.praha-vysehrad.cz), meaning high castle, has an important place in the Czech national psyche. On this rocky mound overlooking the River Vltava, the legendary Přemyslid Princess Libuše foretold the founding of a great city on the banks of the river. She is said to have married a common man and begotten the children who would become the founders of the Czech nation. Unfortunately for the legends, archaeological activity can only date the settlement here to the 10th century, making it younger than Prague Castle.

The castle was built around 1085 by the Přemyslid leader Vratislav II and his two successors, who sought to consolidate power within their growing kingdoms. Along with the castle, an abbey was also built, and later a Romanesque basilica. Power was transferred to Prague Castle by the end of the 12th century. However, Charles IV breathed new life into Vyšehrad with new fortifications and large mansions in homage to his mother, who was descended from the Přemyslid dynasty. During the

Hussite uprising many of the fortifications were destroyed, to be rebuilt in the late 17th century.

From the metro station, a short walk will lead through two gateways and on to a simple stone church. This is **St Martin's Rotunda** (rotunda svatého Martina), one of the oldest churches in Bohemia. Built in the 11th century, it was restored in the late 1800s.

The 11th-century St Martin's Rotunda

Make your way to the neo-Gothic **Basilica of Saints Peter and Paul ㉙** (bazilika svatého Petra a Pavla; daily Apr–Oct 10am–6pm, Nov–Mar 10am–5pm), which was erected on the site of earlier places of worship. At this time, Vyšehrad's mythical status as the birthplace of the Czech nation was once more gaining favour thanks to a blossoming spirit of nationalism. It was decided that the cemetery here would become a **national cemetery** (www.hrbitovy.cz) for illustrious Czechs, a symbol of national pride. The cemetery has some fine sculptures carved by masters of their art, and the composers Antonín Dvořák and Bedřich Smetana, along with the poet Jan Neruda, are among the many Czech luminaries who rest here.

NATIONAL TECHNICAL MUSEUM

The **National Technical Museum ㉚** (Národní Technické muzeum; www.ntm.cz; Tue–Fri 9am–5.30pm, Sat–Sun 10am–6pm; tram

Lying woman, nude, by Rudolf Kremlicka, Trades Fair Palace

routes 1, 8, 12, 25, 26, 51 and 56), hides a wealth of machinery relating to man's technical achievements. There are sections on astronomy, cinematography, industry and mining. However, the main focus of the museum resides in its array of cars, trains and aeroplanes dating from the days when motorised transport was still in its infancy.

THE MUSEUM OF MODERN AND CONTEMPORARY ART

Founded in 1995 in the **Trades Fair Palace** ㉛ (Veletržní palác; www.ngprague.cz; Tue–Sun 10am–6pm; tram routes 1, 5, 12, 17, 24 and 26), a masterpiece of 1920s architecture, the National Gallery's collection of **Modern and Contemporary Art** showcases work from the 19th, 20th and 21st centuries. The redesigned interior of the palace offers a contemporary viewing environment very suited to its collection. Although the works of Czech artists such as Mikoláš Aleš – who was at the forefront of the 'generation of the National Theatre' group – feature prominently, its draw for foreign visitors may well be its French collection.

The collection was brought together with the precise aim of representing the major transitions of French art. Many of the works on show were purchased by the Czech State in the 1920s. Each major modern school or artist figures here, from the Barbizon School to influential Cubist works by Picasso and Braque. The museum also has works by Gauguin, Cézanne and Delacroix, along with a range of Impressionist canvases. In the early 20th century, Prague's influence on the arts, photography and architecture was considerable and the gallery offers an interesting exposition of the exponents of each genre.

THE EXHIBITION GROUND AND STROMOVKA PARK

The **Stromovka** (tram routes 5, 12, 14, 15 and 17) was for many centuries a royal hunting ground before being designated a public park in 1804. Today its woodland and lakes provide a pleasant alternative to the sometimes hot and dusty city streets. The **Exhibition Ground** (Výstaviště) was chosen as the location for the Jubilee of 1891, and its large buildings have been used to host regular exhibitions and concerts. Beside the exhibition halls is **Lapidarium** (www.nm.cz; May–Nov Thu–Sun noon–6pm, Wed 10am–4pm), the National Museum's collection of sculpture. Here you will find some exceptional works, including Petr Parléř's figures from the Old Town Bridge Tower.

MOZART MUSEUM

The **Bertramka Villa** ㉜ (www.bertramka.eu; daily 10am–3pm; Anděl metro station; currently closed for renovation but large groups are permitted with prior arrangement) was where Mozart stayed on numerous occasions during his visits to Prague. It sits on a wooded expanse of land, which in his time would have been quite removed from the hubbub of the city. In 1787 during one of his visits, Mozart composed elements of the opera *Don Giovanni* only hours before the work's debut at the Estates Theatre. The small museum here displays letters and scores in the hand of the great man, along with a number of musical instruments. In summer there are recitals in the courtyard.

LETNÁ PARK

Set on the banks of the Vltava opposite the Jewish Quarter, **Letná Park** (Letenské sady) is another open space within easy reach of the city. It offers superb views upriver and across the Old Town. Visitors are also drawn to a strange modern sculpture that sits on a concrete plinth overlooking the Vltava. The constantly swaying arm of a giant metronome was installed here after the Velvet Revolution, replacing a huge statue of Stalin.

TROJA PALACE

Situated to the north of the city on the banks on the Vltava is the huge **Troja Palace** ❸❸ (Trojský zámek; www.ghmp.cz; Apr–Oct Tue–Sun 10am–6pm, Fri 1–6pm; Holešovice metro station then bus 112). Constructed by the architect Jean-Baptiste Mathey as a summer home for the Sternberg family from 1679–85, the palace became the fashionable place in which to be seen upon its completion. Designed in the classic Italianate style, it has stunning frescoes adorning its interior, the ones in the Grand Hall being particularly impressive. Among the figures depicted are Habsburg emperors Rudolf I and Leopold I. The gardens sloping down to the river were in the French style, an innovation in Prague. The palace now houses the collection of the Prague **City Gallery**, mainly comprising 19th-century Czech painters.

Above the Troja Palace, on the hill that overlooks the river, are the lovely **Prague Botanical Gardens** (www.botanicka.cz; Greenhouse Tue–Sun May–Sept 9am–6pm, Apr and Oct 9am–5pm, Nov–Feb 9am–4pm, Mar 9am–5pm; gardens also open Mon). The most impressive attraction here is the Fata Morgana glasshouse that has a variety of flora from different climatic zones.

A waxwork at the City Transport Museum

BUBENEČ AND STŘEŠOVICE

Just behind the district of Hradčany are Bubeneč and Střešovice. The former comprises large villas and fin-de-siècle apartment blocks, home to diplomats, embassy staff and high-ranking civil servants. Střešovice is similarly bourgeois and home to the **Public Transport Museum** (www.dpp.cz; Apr–Nov Sat–Sun 9am–5pm), with an interesting array of old trams and buses. Just around the corner is the **Müller Villa** (www.mullerovavila.cz; guided tour only, booked in advance; Tue, Thu, Sat and Sun 9am–6pm, the only example of the work of Brno-born Modernist architect Adolf Loos in Prague.

A little further out, in the district of Břevnov, is the park of Obora hvězda. At the centre of the park is the remarkable, six-pointed Renaissance palace known as the **Letohrádek hvězda** (www.pamatniknarodnihopisemnictvi.cz; Apr–Oct 10am–6pm) that has on display a huge model of the Battle of Bílá Hora that took place nearby.

VINOHRADY AND ŽIŽKOV

Take metro line A to Jiřího z Poděbrad station, and you will emerge in the increasingly fashionable, densely built-up quarter of **Vinohrady**, somewhat dingy in places but full of atmosphere and historical charm. Nearby is the Modernist **Church of the Sacred Heart**, built in 1932, which has a distinctive, tombstone-shaped clocktower. Behind the church, turn left on Milešovská Street to be confronted by the gargantuan **Television Tower** (www.towerpark.cz; daily 8am–midnight). Construction began in the communist era and was completed in 1992. For a spectacular view of the city you can ascend 93-metre (305ft) of the 216-metre (709ft) tower to the observation deck

The tower is actually in the neighbouring, and rather more seedy, district of Žižkov, known for its working-class credentials – at one time it was a hotbed of sedition – and vast number of local pubs. The hill that rises to the north of the district is home to the **National Monument ③④**, a large block of granite that houses the Tomb of the Unknown Soldier. On the way up the hill you pass the **Army Museum** (www.vhu.cz; Tue–Sun 10am–6pm; free; currently closed for renovation), with interesting displays on the role of the Czech army during the two world wars.

EXCURSIONS

The area immediately around Prague has a number of places that make fine day trips from the city. It is possible to reach all the sights by public transport and several companies offer a range of morning or day trips by bus.

Karlštejn Castle is a prime example of a medieval fortress

KARLŠTEJN

Rising high above the treetops of the winding valley of the River Berounka like a medieval vision come true, the castle of **Karlštejn** 🟤 is one of the great sights of Bohemia, drawing crowds of visitors. It was begun by Emperor Charles IV in 1348 as a spiritual retreat and repository for the crown jewels and the sacred relics he collected. The castle's present appearance is partly the result of over-zealous rebuilding in the 19th century.

An alternative to the long walk uphill from the village at the foot of the castle is to ride in one of the horse-drawn carriages. From here there is a choice of three tours. Tour I (www. hradkarlstejn.cz; daily July–Aug 9am–6.30pm, Tue–Sun May, June 9am–5.30pm, Apr 9am–5pm, Sept 9.30am–5.30pm, Oct 9.30am–4.30pm, Mar 9.30am–4pm, Nov–Feb 10am–3pm) takes in the imperial palace. Tour II (daily July–Aug 9.05am–6.05pm, except Mon in June; Tue–Sun May and Sept 9.35am–5.05pm, Oct until 4.05pm) reveals the castle's sacred heart, a sequence of gorgeously decorated interiors. They include the Chapel of St Catherine, with wall-paintings set in a matrix of semi-precious stones, and the Chapel of the Holy Cross, with a starry vault and a stunning series of portraits by court painter Master Theodoric. Tour III (daily July–Aug 9.15am–6.15pm, May and Sept 10.15am–5.15pm, Jun Tue–Sun 9.15am–5.15pm) includes the great tower which is Karlštejn's dominant feature. There's also Tour IV, without the accompanying guide, around the Castle Treasure (Jun Tue–Sun 9am–5.30pm, Jul–Aug daily 9am–6.30pm, May, Sep Tue–Sun 9.30am–5.30pm, Oct until 4.30pm, Nov 10am–3pm mid-Nov–Feb Sat–Sun 10am–3pm, closed Jan).

KŘIVOKLÁT

While Karlštejn is a short train ride from Prague, the medieval castle at **Křivoklát** ㊱ (www.krivoklat.cz; Tue–Sun July–Aug 9am–6pm, June and Sept 9am–5pm, May 10am–5pm, mid-Mar–Apr and Oct 10am–4pm, Nov–Dec Sat–Sun 10am–3pm, Jan–mid-Mar Sat 10am–3pm; reservation essential) lies deeper in the countryside, high above a tributary of the Berounka. Surrounded by vast forests, it originated as a royal hunting lodge in the 12th century. Rebuilt and extended, it continued its role as a royal residence and is everything a feudal fortress should be, with sturdy walls and towers frowning down from a commanding height, and authentic medieval interiors.

LIDICE

Following the assassination of Reichsprotektor Heydrich on 27 May 1942, the wrath of the Nazis was turned on an unassuming mining village near the steel town of Kladno. On the night of 9 June, **Lidice** ㊲ was sealed off, its menfolk shot and its women

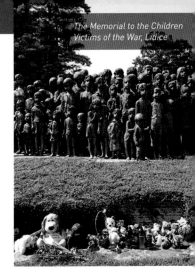

and children sent to concentration camps, from which few returned. The village was bulldozed and its name erased from the record. After the war, a new Lidice was built a short distance away and the site of the original village became a memorial, with a rose garden of remembrance and a **museum** (www.lidice-memorial.cz; daily Apr–Oct 9am–6pm, Mar 9am–5pm, Nov–Feb 9am–4pm) telling the tragic story in bitter detail.

NELAHOZEVES

On the banks of the Vltava north of Prague, the otherwise ordinary village of **Nelahozeves** ❸ has not one, but two attractions, albeit of very different kinds. Music-lovers make their way to the **Dvořák Birthplace Museum** (Památník Antonína Dvořáka; www.nm.cz; 1st and 3rd weeks in the month Wed–Sun 9.30am–noon and 1–5pm, 2nd and 4th weeks in the month Wed–Fri 9.30am–noon and 1–5pm), the modest village house where the great composer was born, while rather more visitors head for the **zámek** (www.zameknelahozeves.cz; Tue–Sun 9am–5pm). After the fall of Communism, this splendid Renaissance castle was given back to its original owners, the princely Lobkowicz family, who completed its restoration. Begun in the mid-16th century, the castle is extravagantly sgraffitoed on the outside and has a succession of opulent interiors reflecting the high status of what was one of the kingdom's leading families.

MĚLNÍK

Visible from far away across the plain, the castle and church of the little town of **Mělník** ❸ crown the bluff high above the confluence of the Vltava with the Elbe (Labe). With its origins in the 9th century, the castle was the place where the future 'Good King' Wenceslas (born around 907) was tutored in the ways of Christianity by his grandmother, Princess Ludmila. During the 14th century, Charles IV revived the local wine industry by importing vines from Burgundy, and, stepping down in terraces from the castle, Mělník's vineyards are still famous, and the wine is on sale in the castle shop. The **zámek** (www.lobkowicz-melnik.cz; Apr–Oct daily 9.30am–6pm) is in a variety of styles ranging from Gothic to Baroque, and has interesting wine cellars. Nearby, the parish church with its landmark tower has a *kostnice* (ossuary).

Mělník

TEREZÍN AND LITOMĚŘICE

Within sight of each other, and only separated by the River Labe, the towns of **Terezín** ❹ and **Litoměřice** could hardly be more different. For centuries the market centre for the fertile surrounding countryside, historic Litoměřice was one of Bohemia's most important towns, with a vast central square and a wealth of churches. By contrast, Terezín is an ugly upstart, a grim fortress town of barrack blocks, laid out in the late 18th century to protect the northern approaches to Prague. Outside the main walls and moats, the **Small Fortress** (Malá pevnost; www.pamatnik-terezin.cz; daily Apr–Oct 8am–6pm, Nov–Mar 8am–4.30pm) served as a political prison in Austro-Hungarian times. The regime was brutal, but nothing like what was to come under the Nazis. In 1941 they expelled all Terezín's inhabitants, and turned the town into what they claimed was a model ghetto. No extermination camp, Terezín nevertheless saw thousands of deaths, and a majority of those incarcerated here were eventually transported to Auschwitz. The **Ghetto Museum** (daily Apr–Oct 9am–6pm, Nov–Mar 9am–5.30pm) brings home the horror of the place as well as celebrating the unquenchable spirit which made it a centre of creative endeavour, however temporary.

KOLÍN

Due east of Prague, **Kolín** ❹ is a rather nondescript industrial town on the banks of the River Labe. However, it makes a convenient stopping point on the way to or from Kutná Hora, and has a fine main square with a Renaissance town hall as well as the splendid Gothic **Church of St Bartholomew**, the glorious choir of which was the work of Petr Parléř.

The name of the town's most famous son is held in high esteem by brass-band fans all around the world: Czech bandmasters had a virtual monopoly on Austro-Hungarian military bands, and supreme among them was František Kmoch, born here in 1848. His memory is honoured every year in June, when enthusiasts from around the world converge on Kolín and the air is filled with the cheerful sound of trumpets, trombones and tubas.

KUTNÁ HORA

On high ground overlooking a winding river valley, this old town was at its peak in the Middle Ages, when it was bigger than London, and the silver extracted from its mines underpinned the prosperity of Prague and the Bohemian royal court. When the silver ran out, the town shrank to less than a third of its former size and became a backwater. There is still plenty of evidence of **Kutná Hora's** ⓬ great days; enough to make it one of the most popular day trips from the capital.

The outstanding monument is **St Barbara's Cathedral** (Chrám sv. Barbora; www.khfarnost.cz; daily, Apr–Oct 9am–6pm, Mar and Nov–Dec 10am–5pm, Jan–Feb 10am–4pm). Despite its incomplete state, this is one of the glories of Central European Gothic architecture. Begun at the end of the 14th century, in the mid-16th century it was given its extraordinary roof in the form of a triple tent by Benedikt Ried, who also designed the beautiful vaulting of the nave.

On one side of the street running north from the cathedral is the huge **Jesuit College**, on the other, above the drop to the river, a line of Baroque sculptures of gesticulating saints. Further along the valley rim, the 15th-century palace known as the **Hradek** contains a museum of silver, while beyond rises the tower of another major church, **St James** (sv. Jakub). Adjacent to the church is the much-restored power-house of the city's medieval economy, the **Italian Court** (Vlašský dvůr; www.guideskutnahora.com; daily Apr–Sept 9am–6pm, Mar and Oct 10am–5pm, Nov–Feb 10am–4pm), now housing a museum of minting. It was here that experts brought in from Florence turned out coins like the Prague *groschen*, legal tender over much of the known world until the 19th century.

In the suburb of Sedlec just northeast of the town, next to a Gothic church made Baroque by the architect Santini, stands one of the country's great curiosities, the **Ossuary** (Kostnice; www.ossuary.eu; Apr–Sept Mon–Sat 8am–6pm, Sun 9am–6pm, Oct and Mar 9am–5pm, Nov–Feb 9am–4pm), containing a fantastical array of bells, coats of arms and chandeliers, all made from human bones.

PRŮHONICE

Only 16km (10 miles) from Prague, the village of **Průhonice** ⓱ is famous for its castle and vast landscaped park. The castle (www.zamekpruhonice.cz, not normally open to the public) is occupied by the Botanical Institute of the National Academy of Science, whose botanists have a wonderful array of trees, shrubs and other plants at their disposal in the vast park where they work.

The Ossuary, Kutna Hora

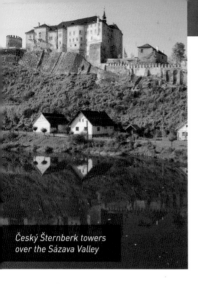
Český Šternberk towers over the Sázava Valley

Průhonice Castle dates to the Middle Ages, but the present building is a romantic structure in Czech neo-Renaissance style. It was built in the late 19th century by Count Ernst Silva-Taroucca, who was also responsible for laying out the park (www.pruhonickypark.cz; daily May–Sept 7am–8pm, Apr and Oct 7am–7pm, Mar 7am–6pm, Nov–Feb 8am–5pm), a major achievement of landscape design, with lakes, vistas, walks, an alpine garden and, above all, countless trees, both native and exotic.

KONOPIŠTĚ

The Czech Republic's main motorway connecting Prague to Brno and beyond leads beyond the tatty outer suburbs into attractive countryside rich in parks and castles. Close to the town of Benešov is **Konopiště** ❹ (www.zamek-konopiste.cz; May, Sept 10am–4pm, Jun–Aug 10am–5pm, Oct 10am–3pm, Nov Sat–Sun 10am–3pm). It rivals Karlštejn in its popularity with visitors. Originally a medieval stronghold built in the 13th century, it was restored and modernised in the late 19th century by Archduke Franz Ferdinand. Redolent of the last days of the Austro-Hungarian Empire, the interiors seem much as they were lived in by the archduke and his family, while the pervasive decoration with hunting trophies reflects his passion for the chase. A particular highlight is the armoury, one of the finest private collections in the world. Franz Ferdinand re-landscaped the castle park, providing it with a lavish rose garden.

ČESKÝ ŠTERNBERK

While Konopiště is buried deep in woodland, the castle at **Český Šternberk** 45 (www.hradceskysternberk.cz; June–Aug Tue–Sun 9am–6pm, May and Sept Tue–Sun 9am–5pm, Apr and Oct Sat–Sun 9am–5pm) sits on a rocky ridge high above the River Sázava, seemingly impregnable against all comers. The castle was begun in the mid-13th century by a member of the Šternberk family, one of the most powerful dynasties in the realm. It has been greatly remodelled over the years and in its present form is a largely Baroque structure. Under Communism, a Šternberk was allowed to stay on as curator. Today, the restored stronghold is worth a visit for its superb site and its fascinating, often oddly shaped interiors. It is filled with furnishings and fittings in styles ranging from Renaissance to Empire, as well as portraits, hunting trophies, chandeliers and artefacts from the Thirty Years' War, when the castle survived a couple of sieges.

Rural retreat

Cold-shouldered at the imperial court in Vienna because he had married Sophie Chotek, a mere countess, Franz Ferdinand was happy to hide away in his rural retreat at Konopiště, where he is reckoned to have shot animals by the hundred thousand. He himself perished by the bullet, when he and Sophie were assassinated in Sarajevo in June 1914 by a Serb nationalist, in what is generally considered to be the starting signal for World War I.

A performance by the
Prague State Opera Ballet

WHAT TO DO

Prague is bursting at the seams with things to do, even after the museums and galleries have shut. Highbrow pursuits rival opportunities for more frivolous entertainment. Whether you choose to bask in the city's rich musical heritage or simply enjoy a glass of pilsner in one of its legendary beer cellars, this is one city where there really is something for everyone.

ENTERTAINMENT

Prague is home to a multitude of theatre, ballet and opera companies, with a strong tradition of puppetry and mime. However, it is undoubtedly in the field of classical music that it has established itself as a world leader, as its wealth of concert venues and its packed musical programme will testify.

MUSIC AND THEATRE

The city has been a major concert venue for at least five centuries. It greeted the premiere of Mozart's *Don Giovanni* and played host to numerous major composers during their careers. Large concert halls have been built during various periods in the history of Prague and today, along with a host of smaller venues, they provide a welcoming home for concerts all year long.

The city is home to some very fine classical ensembles, foremost of which is the **Czech Philharmonic Orchestra** (www.ceskafilharmonie.cz), one of the finest in the world. Others include the **Prague Symphony Orchestra** (www.fok.cz) and the **Prague Radio Symphony Orchestra** (www2.rozhlas.cz/socr). These, and touring ensembles, appear at venues such as the **Rudolfinum** (www.rudolfinum.cz, tel: 227 059 227) or

Smetana Hall at the Municipal House (www.obecnidum.cz, tel: 222 002 101). Lesser-known touring outfits or smaller groups, for example quartets, often perform at the **Clementinum** or **St Nicholas Church** to name a couple of venues.

Throughout the year large-scale festivals devote themselves to the work of particular composers or specific musical styles. The best of these are the **Prague Spring** (www.festival.cz) and **Prague Autumn**. Favoured composers include Czech heroes such as Dvořák and Smetana and hearing their music in their homeland is an experience not to be forgotten.

Concerts are held at lunchtime and in the evening and you can purchase seats from the ticket sellers in Old Town Square. Alternatively, head to the box office of the venue in question. With ticket prices representing such good value there is the potential

⊙ KAFKA, BACK IN THE LIMELIGHT

Like a great number of the central figures in the history of Prague, Franz Kafka spoke German. This factor lost him the support of the Czech public when the country rid itself once and for all of Austro-Hungarian state supervision in 1918, and again in 1945 when the German minority was expelled. The author of *The Castle*, *The Trial* and *Metamorphosis* was equally banished by the communist regime for being a bourgeois intellectual.

But Kafka is firmly back in fashion. The place of his birth at U Radnice 5 bears his name, and a small exhibition (Tue–Fri 10am–6pm, Sat 10am–5pm) reveals his life and work. The more ambitious Franz Kafka museum (Cihelná 2b; www.kafka museum.cz; daily 10am–6pm) uses multimedia displays to explore the writer's background, emphasising the influence of personal experiences on his books.

to see a different performance each day – and many
people do just that.

It is cheaper to buy
tickets for events from the
box office concerned, but
if that proves impossible
tickets are usually available via Ticketpro (www.
ticketpro.cz) from numer-
ous points around the city,
including all the Prague
Information Service
offices (see page 131),
Bohemia Ticket (www.
bohemiaticket.cz) at K + K

Dvořák's works top the bill
in Prague's concert halls

Hotel Fenix, Ve Smečkách 30, and at Ticketpro itself in the
Lucerna Passage off Wenceslas Square.

The city is also home to the Czech National Theatre, ballet and opera companies, and regularly welcomes touring
groups. The **National Theatre** (tel: 224 901 448; www.narod
nidivadlo.cz) is an enormous complex with several stages,
and encompasses the national opera and ballet companies.
It also includes the **Laterna Magika** (tel: 224 901 417), one
of the major European troupes and at the forefront of multimedia theatre. This popular genre blends music, mime,
ballet, surrealism and satire into a powerful melange that
transcends the language barrier. Each season, **Estates
Theatre** (tel: 224 901448; www.narodnidivadlo.cz) also plays
host to several companies, and the **State Opera** (tel: 224 227
266; www.czechopera.cz) stages seminal opera, ballet and
dance productions.

Marionette performances take place at the **National Marionette Theatre** (tel: 224 819 322; www.mozart.cz). You can watch the puppets run the gamut of emotions in sophisticated plays of a more serious bent, or clown around in light-hearted pieces.

Useful listings of what's on during your stay in the city can be found on the website www.ceskakultura.cz and are included in the English-language *Prague Post* newspaper (www.prague post.com).

NIGHTLIFE

If cultural overload strikes, why not seek refuge in Prague's plethora of bars and cafés where you can enjoy a few drinks and listen to live rock, jazz or folk music. For a glass of local beer head for one of the city's huge beer cellars. However, on a warm summer's evening, try to find a bar terrace with a view over the city.

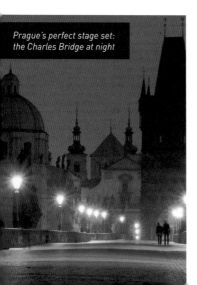

Prague's perfect stage set: the Charles Bridge at night

A city that is so famous for its beer has to be a good place to have a drink and a pub or beer hall can be a convivial place to spend an evening. For well-kept beer and cosy surroundings try **U Hrocha** (Thunovská 10) and **U Kocoura** (Nerudova 2), both in Malá Strana, or the rather touristy **U Zlatého tygra** (Husova 17; www.uzlatehotygra.cz) in the Old Town or **Zlý časy** (Čestmírova 5; http://zly casy.eu). Perhaps surprisingly Prague is also home to number of chic cocktail bars including **Cloud 9** (Hilton Prague, Pobřežní 1; www.cloud9.cz) with breathtaking views over the city, **Bugsy's** (Pařížská 10; www.bugsysbar. cz), **Tretter's** (V kolkovně 3; www.tretters.cz) and **Ocean Drive** (V kolkovně 7). Žižkov is famous for its pubs and the suitably loud and seedy

Tretter's New York Bar

U vystřelenýho oka (U božích bojovníků 3; www.uvoka.cz) is a good place to get a feel for the area.

As the evening wears on, Prague's lively nightlife kicks in. Trends can be short-lived, so keep an eye on the local press or websites such as www.techno.cz for the most popular club nights. For a relatively safe bet head for Prague's most long-standing club, **Radost FX** (Bělehradská 120; http://radostfx.cz). Still very stylish, this venue attracts the cream of the local DJs, not to mention international guest DJs, and holds a gay night once a week. Other places you might want to check out include the popular and well-dressed **Celnice** (V celnici 4), **Mecca** (U Průhonu 3; www.mecca.cz) that also holds jazz nights, and **Roxy** (Dlouhá 33; www.roxy.cz) for house and R&B.

While the Prague gay and lesbian scene is fairly small there are some good venues to check out. The long-established mixed bar **Friends** (Bartolomějská 11; www.friendsclub.cz) is a good place to start, as is **21 Klub** (Římská 21; www.klub21.cz). Clubs to try include the mixed **TERmix** (Třebízského 4a; www.club-termix.cz) or the gay **Alcatraz** (Krakovská 19; http://mujalkac.webnode.cz).

SHOPPING

The last three decades have seen huge changes in how and where people shopped in the city. This is one area where Prague has completely broken away from its communist past of limited goods in state-owned department stores. Today, shopping here is an experience much like that in any other European city, with an array of quality goods and traditional handicrafts.

The main shopping streets boast the flagship stores of all the well-known, international chains. However, by venturing into the Old Town you will come across small, specialist shops.

Do remember to check whether stores take credit cards. Although payment by credit card is widespread, it is by no means universally accepted.

WHERE TO SHOP

The majority of the souvenir shops can be found along the 'royal way' leading from Municipal House through the Old Town Square, and in Lesser Quarter Square across the river. Big names

A shop window in the Old Town sparkles crystal

from the (Western) high street have set up shop around Wenceslas Square and along Na příkopě, whereas on the more up-market streets of Pařížská and Jungmannova, European haute couture rubs shoulders with the emerging Czech designer labels.

A good place to shop for souvenirs is the Týn Court (Týnský dvůr or Ungelt), just behind the Týn Church. Here you'll find books, fashion items, wines to taste, and cafés and restaurants in which to take a break.

Shoppers in the Old Town

WHAT TO BUY

The Czech Republic has a reputation for the quality of its traditional products. Glasswear and porcelain are particularly renowned and examples of both are to be found in royal collections across Europe. **Bohemian Crystal** is an exclusive brand name despite having factories scattered throughout the country. Lead crystal ranges in lead content from 14 percent to 24 percent and comes in myriad shapes and patterns. Traditional decanters, vases, bowls and glasses, with patterns cut by hand, make pretty souvenirs or gifts and are to be had at roughly half the price of that in other European countries.

More modern designs in **glasswear** are also popular, from large, decorative sculptures to vases. Bunches of large glass flowers mimic the shape of fresh blooms.

The delicate features of Bohemian **porcelain** figurines have changed little in the past 200 years, and their flowing forms are highly prized among collectors. The best originate from small factories around Karlovy Vary, but they can also be bought in Prague. The Český Porcelán factory on the outskirts of town – which also has an outlet on site – is famous for its dinner services in its signature cobalt blue 'onion' design.

Prague has a reputation as being a **city of the arts**. There are numerous stalls selling – often rather dodgy – watercolours or line drawings of Prague. Moody black-and-white photographs offer yet another perspective of the city. Apart from these more obvious offerings, Prague also has several galleries selling works by both established and up-and-coming artists. For something a bit different have a look at the Cubist and Modernist replicas on sale at the **Kubista** (www.kubista.cz) and **Modernista** (www.modernista.cz) shops.

There are also a number of **antiques dealers**, with glass and porcelain being particularly prevalent. As a leading city of the Habsburg Empire, Prague counted a large number of wealthy and cosmopolitan citizens. These collections, along with a rich legacy of Bohemian furniture and artefacts, form the basis of today's trade in antiques.

Garnets have been mined and polished in the

Cubist replica furniture at Kubista

Czech Republic for centuries, and the pretty, semiprecious stones can be bought in jewellers across the city.

Shops selling **Czech handicrafts** (try Manufaktura; www.manufaktura.cz) are often enticingly set in historic houses or converted cellars. Wooden **toys** make good presents for young children. **Ceramics** come in a variety of shapes and sizes, decorated with glazes made of earth pigments. In the Czech Republic, **decorated eggs** feature prominently in Easter celebrations and are widely available as souvenirs – coloured ribbons are attached so that you can hang them in your home. **Marionettes** make an original souvenir and come in a range of characters. The craft stalls of Josefov are appropriately laden with Rabbis. Finally, **basketwear** can be excellent although unfortunately the most beautiful items are often the largest and too bulky for the return flight home.

In a city where performances of classical **music** will feature prominently during your stay, it comes as no surprise that music is readily available, with some stores selling a huge range of classical recordings. CDs are inexpensive and look out especially for those of works by Smetana and Dvořák.

Bottles of the Czech pilsner **beer** are rather heavy to take home, but try a bottle of the heady Becherovka liqueur. Plum brandy or *slivovice* is also widely available, as are brandies distilled from other fruits.

SPORTS AND ACTIVITIES

Spectator sports: Sparta Praha is the Czech Republic's top football team. They play in a stadium (tel: 296 111 400; www.sparta.cz) adjacent to Letná Park and their season runs from September to April. **Ice hockey** is extremely popular, the main venue being HC Slavia's O2 Arena stadium (tel: 266 771 351; www.o2arena.cz). The Czechs are naturally proud of the number of professional **tennis** players they have produced in recent decades. The National Tennis facility (www. cltk.cz) on Štvanice Island below the Hlávkův Bridge hosts Grand Prix tournaments.

Swimming: There are a number of pools in Prague. Plavecký stadion Podolí (Podolská 74; tel: 241 433 952; www.pspodoli.cz) is the largest pool complex in the city with two outdoor pools, one inside, diving boards and a waterslide. Aquacentrum Letňany Lagoon (Tupolevova 665; tel: 283 921 799; www. letnanylagoon.cz) has good safe areas for children.

☉ RIDES AND CRUISES

Apart from walking there are a variety of different ways of seeing the city. Horse-drawn carriages carry you at a gentle pace through the cobbled streets of the Old Town; or opt for a ride in a vintage car; open-top, weather permitting. Both tours depart from Old Town Square.

Riverboats operating day or evening cruises ply the waters of the Vltava, with candlelit dinners and jazz bands for added interest. Boarding takes place on the Lesser Quarter bank just below Charles Bridge. See the website of the two best-known companies for details: the Steam Navigation Society of Prague (www.paroplavba.cz) and Pražské Benátky (www. prazskebenatky.cz).

During the summer months (April to mid-November, weekends and holidays), Prague's historic tram 41 (www. dpp.cz) tours the city. The National Theatre, Malostranské náměstí and Wenceslas Square are all boarding points.

CHILDREN'S PRAGUE

At first glance Prague seems to have little to offer children, the accent of a typical tour being on visiting the major churches, palaces and galleries. However, there are a few fun activities that will keep children happy and maybe even amuse parents.

Transport can be entertaining. Ride in a horse-drawn carriage through the streets of the Old Town. Boat trips on the Vltava are also fun; take some bread to feed the ducks and swans. A simple ride on a tram can be a great experience in itself, and taking the funicular railway up to Petřín Hill is thrilling for children.

With a little advance planning, a well-chosen **theatre trip** can be a stimulating experience even for small children. The Lanterna Magika features dance, mime and the use of lighting effects. The National Marionette Theatre (tel: 224 819 322;

One of Prague's numerous puppet theatres

www.mozart.cz) stages shows for all ages, including a puppet version of *Don Giovanni*.

If your child is mad about **funfairs**, a large one comes to the Prague Exhibition Ground during the summer months.

Child-friendly **museums** include the National Technical Museum, with plenty of interactive displays. The National Museum has collections of tropical insects and animal bones – children might be enthralled by the giant insects. The Toy Museum in the eastern part of Prague Castle will appeal with its large selection of toys from ancient Greece to the present day. Time your visit to coincide with the hourly changing of the guards in the first courtyard – most impressive at noon.

Kids love the **Mirror Maze** on Petřín Hill, although younger children may find it frightening. Bite-sized lunchtime **concerts**, held at venues across town, can be a great way of introducing children to classical music.

CALENDAR OF EVENTS

Prague's cultural calendar is an extremely busy and ever-changing one, and as such impossible to give full details of here. For up-to-date listings and information, the *Prague Post* is the best source. However, as a guide and to help you plan your trip, here are some of the major annual events taking place both in the city and across the country.

May Prague International Marathon (dates vary from year to year).

May–June Prague Spring Festival (Pražské jaro; www.festival.cz): one of the world's best classical-music festivals, with performances by celebrated musicians at major venues throughout the city.

June Smetana National Opera Festival (Litomyšl; http://festival.smetana-litomysl.com). Festival of the Five-petalled Rose (www.slavnostipetilis teruze.eu): falconry, fire-throwing and target-jousting in Český Krumlov. Tanec Praha Contemporary Dance Festival (www.tanecpraha.cz): foreign and Czech dancers collaborate.

July Rock for People Festival: open-field music concerts (www.rockfor people.cz). International Film Festival at Karlovy Vary (www.kviff.com). Summer Festivities of Early Music (www.letnislavnosti.cz).

July–August Italian Opera Festival. Displays of music and dance in traditional costume.

August The Chopin Music Festival (www.chopinfestival.cz): held at venues throughout Bohemia.

September–October Live Cafés (Kavárny naživo; http://kavarnynazivo.cz) concerts, theatre performances, and other art projects in various cafés thorought the city.

October International Jazz Festival Praha (www.jazzfestivalpraha.com).

November Prague Writers' Festival (www.pwf.cz): talks and book signings with internationally renowned authors. Prague German-language Theatre Festival (www.theater.cz).

December Advent and Christmas-time activities such as craft markets, carol concerts and an open-air arts festival.

31 December Spectacular New Year celebrations across the city.

EATING OUT

Czech food offers the perfect antidote to the rigours of healthy eating and nouvelle cuisine: honest, filling, often delicious dishes, based on the kind of recipes grandmother kept to herself. You will also find that prices are still relatively low, and it is possible to eat well for around £10 ($16) per person, although the finest establishments charge significantly more.

Since the Velvet Revolution, Prague has become one of the busiest tourist cities in Europe, and some international chefs and restaurateurs have been quick to take advantage of the new opportunities and charge accordingly. There is a surprising amount of international cuisine available, from sushi to Indian curries.

WHERE TO EAT

Prague is generously endowed with places to eat, and now that restaurants no longer have to be licensed by the state; many new establishments have opened as international influences find a foothold in the country. Apart from conventional restaurants (restaurace), which may be exclusive or geared to a regional or foreign cuisine, the following options are worth seeking out:

Vinárny (wine restaurants – on signs you will see the word Vinárna) may have the same menus as ordinary restaurants but place a special emphasis on their wine list. The ambience is often intimate, and possibly historic.

Pivnice or hospody (pubs or taverns) specialise in draught beer and a limited selection of traditional meat platters. The mood is likely to be jolly and the service informal.

Kavárny (cafés) are essentially for snacks and sweet pastries, although you may find some hot meals on the menu. On signs you will see the word Kavárna. If you are in a rush and in need of a quick bite, there is a wide range of cheap fast-food outlets and self-service bistros in the city centre.

The atmosphere in Prague's eateries is often colourful or romantic, although the standard of service varies. Most waiters will understand a few English phrases, and some will undoubtedly speak very good English; however, learning a few words of Czech will certainly be appreciated. Terrace cafés

Inside one of Prague's many kavárny (cafés)

and restaurants help to minimise the problem. If a restaurant becomes busy it is normal practice for diners to share a table – many pubs have long communal tables that seat 10 or 12 people.

Be aware of the hidden charges added by some eateries and pubs. A cover charge of around 30 Kč per person may be added to the bill. Some budget cafés charge for condiments, while others leave appetisers on the table without telling you that there is a charge for them. Pubs often send waiters out with trays of short drinks, but any drinks you consume will be added to your bill, although these charges will be minimal.

BREAKFAST

Breakfast *(snídaně)* is served by hotels from about 6am to 10.30am. In most establishments this will be presented in the form of a buffet, its lavishness depending on the class of the hotel. There will always be tea and coffee, a choice of cereals,

A variety of tempting dishes

cold meats, cheese, eggs, yoghurt and fruit. Check whether the price of breakfast is included in the room rate. If not, there is the option of eating out at one of the American-style diners.

CZECH CUISINE

On weekdays, most Czechs eat early – generally at around 7pm – then head to bed in preparation for the working day ahead. However, restaurants in Prague stay open until around 10pm or 11pm, and even later at weekends, when locals go out to enjoy themselves.

Most restaurants post a printed menu *(jídelní lístek)* near the door, giving you at least an idea of their prices. Nowadays, most cheap, medium-priced and first-class restaurants tend to have menus in English and German as well as Czech.

A menu might be divided into the following categories: *studená jídla* (cold dishes), *polévky* (soups), *teplé předkrmy* (warm starters), *ryby* (fish), *drůbež* (poultry), *hotová jídla* (main courses), and *moučníky* (desserts). A growing number of establishments are offering set meals at lunchtime and in the evening in addition to à la carte.

Try a starter of Prague ham (*Pražská šunka*), a succulent local speciality. It might come served in thin slices, garnished with cucumber and horseradish; with cheese in miniature sandwiches; or folded into horns and stuffed with cream or cream cheese and horseradish.

Soup is a popular choice at both lunch (*oběd*) and dinner (*večeře*). Either a fairly light bouillon or, as is more likely, a thick, wholesome soup of potatoes, vegetables and perhaps some meat. A spoonful of whipped cream may also be added. One of the heartiest traditional recipes is *bramborová polévka s houbami* (potato soup with mushrooms). This thick soup flavoured with onion, bacon, carrots, cabbage, parsley and spices can constitute a meal in itself.

The hearty Czech cuisine typically centres on well-roasted pork or beef with thick gravy. This is supplemented with poultry, game or fish dishes – owing to the tradition of seasonal hunting in the surrounding countryside. The generally heavy, savoury food goes down

A traditional restaurant in Nové Město

The Czechs love their pork

best with cold Czech beer, a brew long held in high esteem by gourmets everywhere.

Meat forms the backbone of Czech cuisine. Always thoroughly cooked, it can be roasted or grilled. The succulent *Pražská hovězí pečeně* (Prague roast beef), a joint of beef stuffed with fried diced ham, peas, egg, onion and spices, is one of the most popular dishes. Also look out for *svíčková pečeně na smetaně*, tasty beef in a cream sauce.

Another gourmet favourite is *Šunka po staročesku* (boiled ham), with a sauce of plums, prunes, walnut kernels and wine. For a taste of the Austro-Hungarian Empire, you should sample some *gulaš* (goulash), a stew flavoured with paprika, or *smažený řízek* (Wiener schnitzel), a delicious breaded veal escalope. Poultry and game are also popular, and depending on the season you will find duck, goose, boar and venison on the menu.

As an accompaniment, pride of place goes to the dumpling. Either made from bread (*houskové knedlíky*, relatively light) or potato (*bramborové knedlíky*, heavier in texture) you will usually find one or two sliced dumplings on your plate. Vegetables have always played a secondary role in traditional cuisine, and when they do appear in soups and stews seem overcooked. You will often see 'stewed vegetables' on menus in English, which forewarns you that they will definitely not be arriving *al dente*. Sauerkraut (*kyselé zelí*) is the most commonly served – red or white cabbage cooked to a melting consistency in animal fat, sugar and a little wine.

Desserts usually figure in the heavyweight category, for example the tasty jablkový *závin* (apple strudel), with a topping of whipped cream. A slightly more delicate variation, *jablka v županu* (apple baked in flaky pastry) uses whole apples stuffed with sugar, cinnamon and raisins. Svestkové *knedlíky* (plum dumplings) are sprinkled with cheese curd and sugar, and then doused in melted butter. A firm favourite is palačinka, ice cream or cream and fruit enveloped in a pancake. Finally, *zmrzlina* (ice cream) or *kompot* (stewed fruit) – sometimes laced with fruit brandy – are old stand-bys.

VEGETARIAN COOKING

The presence of a large expatriate community has led to the emergence of

Prague's Havelská Market is crammed with fresh produce

Czech beer has a reputation to be envied

several vegetarian cafés and restaurants over the past few years. Consequently, many non-vegetarian restaurants now offer a range of options *bez masa* (without meat). One of the best places for vegetarian food is Estrella (Opatovická 159/17, tel: 777 431 344; www.estrellarestaurant.cz; Mon–Sun 11.30am–3.30pm and 6–10pm), which serves excellent, good-value vegetarian fare.

SNACKS

Prague is an ideal place for inexpensive snacks or lunch on the move, bought from one of the city's street stands. A *bramborák* is a savoury potato pancake served on a square of paper, delicious despite the greasy fingers. *Pečená klobása* (roasted sausage) rates a paper plate, a slice of rye bread and a squirt of mild mustard – but no fork or knife. They also come hot-dog-style with onions and mustard. *Smažený sýr* is a kind of vegetarian Wienerschnitzel consisting of a slice of fried cheese.

Chlebíčky, or open sandwiches with a variety of toppings, are also popular in snack bars. You may be offered them if you are invited to a Czech home. American-style fast-food outlets are plentiful, particularly around Wenceslas Square, and more popular with young Czechs than the traditional snack outlets. Gorgeous ice cream is sold everywhere.

DRINKS

Prague offers a wonderful selection of places to drink, of which a large number also serve light meals, and its architectural wealth ensures a range of superb settings. In addition to this, the city has recently started to witness the re-emergence of the thriving café society of the early 20th century.

Czech beer *(pivo)* has a reputation to be envied, and the intense brewing activity in the city of Plzeň (Pilsen) has given the world the *pilsner* style of lager, imitated by many other countries.

⊙ THE ART OF DRINKING

Beer halls are a veritable institution in Bohemia, so much so that some unwritten rules of conduct have evolved over the centuries. This special brand of etiquette dictates that if a man and a woman arrive at a pub together, the man should always enter before the woman in case there is a brawl going on inside.

Never bother the waiter, and ask for his assistance before moving any of the chairs. Place a beer mat on the table to indicate that you are ready to order. Don't tip too much (a few crowns will do) or you'll be seen as arrogant. Always raise your glass to your neighbours before drinking and look them square in the eye. And finally, never complain that your beer has too much of a head – it's the local custom.

Viticulture

Although Bohemia produces some excellent wines, the Czech Republic's best vintages tend to come from Moravia, in the country's east, where the gentle slopes enjoy better sunshine, producing sweeter grapes. To be sure of buying a good bottle, seek advice from a reputable merchant, such as Cellarius in the Lucerna arcade (www.cellarius.cz).

Naturally, local people are adamant that no other beer tastes quite the same because Plzeň beer gets its distinctive flavour from the alkaline water and the excellence of its hops, a key ingredient, which grow on vast wood-and-wire frames in the Bohemian countryside. The most famous beers are *Pilsner Urquell* from Plzeň, Budweiser *Budvar* from České Budějovice (Budweis) and *Staropramen* from Prague.

Other well-regarded breweries abound in Prague and the smaller surrounding towns. Several pubs brew their own light *(světle)* or dark *(tmave)* blends, including U Flekŭ which has been in operation since 1499. All Czech beer is tasty and refreshing but it might be wise to bear in mind that it is probably stronger than what you are used to drinking at home.

Czech **wine** *(víno)* is virtually unknown abroad, so it's likely that you will discover something new and pleasing without having to search very hard. Bohemia produces only a small proportion of the country's total wine output: most of it comes from Moravia. White is *bílé* and red is *červené*.

A drink local to Karlovy Vary, *becherovka* is made of herbs and served chilled as an aperitif, as is the powerful, sweetish *stará myslivecká*. After-dinner drinks generally take the form of fruit brandies (or schnapps), especially *slivovice* which is made from plums.

TO HELP YOU ORDER

May I see the menu? **Mohu vidět jídelní lístek?**
Can I have it without...? **Mohu mít bez...?**
I am a vegetarian. **Jsem vegeterián(ka).** (m/f)
The bill, please. **Zaplatím.**
I'd like... **Prosím...**

beer **pivo**	meat **maso**
bread **chleba**	the menu **jídelní lístek**
butter **máslo**	milk **mléko**
cheese **sýr**	mineral water **minerálku**
coffee **kávu**	salad **salát**
dessert **moučník**	sugar **cukr**
egg **vejce**	tea **čaj**
ice cream **zmrzlinu**	wine **vino**

MENU READER

bažant pheasant	**kapr** carp
brambory potatoes	**klobása** sausage
drůbež poultry	**knedlíky** dumplings
fazole beans	**králík** rabbit
houby mushrooms	**kuře** chicken
hovězí beef	**květák** cauliflower
hrášek peas	**kyselé zelí** sauerkraut
hrozny grapes	**ledvinky** kidneys
hrušky pears	**rajske jablka** tomatoes
husa goose	**špenát** spinach
jablka apples	**šrnčí** venison
jahody strawberries	**štika** pike
játra liver	**šunka** ham
jazyk tongue	**telecí** veal
jehněčí lamb	**telecí brzlík** sweetbreads
kachna duck	**vepřové** pork

PLACES TO EAT

We have used the following symbols to give an idea of the price for a three-course meal for one, excluding wine:

€€€€€	over Kč1,000
€€€€	Kč700–1000
€€€	Kč500–700
€€	Kč300–500
€	under Kč300

OLD TOWN AND NEW TOWN

Bellevue €€€€€ *Smetanovo nábřeží 18, tel: 222 221 443*, www.bellevue restaurant.cz. True to its name, the elegant Bellevue delivers a remarkable view of the Vltava River and Prague Castle from the small square to the south of the Charles Bridge. It serves interesting modern European food. Dishes such as roast veal loin with mushroom sauce are backed up by equally memorable desserts. It also has a vegetarian menu. Open daily noon–3pm and 5.30pm–11pm.

Bílá Kráva €€€€ *Rubešova 10, tel: 224 239 570*, www.bilakrava.cz. On a street tucked behind the National Museum, the 'White Cow' owes its name to the occupation of its owner, who doubles as a cattle farmer in Burgundy, France. Most of the dishes use meat from his herd, flown directly into Prague, but a variety of seafood and lamb dishes also have their place on the menu. A wood-beamed, cottage-like interior complements an ambitious menu that ranges from *escargots* in red wine to *bœuf bourguignon*. Open Mon–Fri 11.30am–11pm, Sat 5–11pm.

Chez Marcel €€ *Haštalská 12, tel: 222 315 676,* www.chezmarcel.cz. Very French, even down to the occasionally grumpy service, and good value, this bistro opposite St Agnes's Convent has all the expected dishes (omelettes, steak and salads), plus French wines by the glass. Tasty, simple food of the sort that is typical in France. Open daily 11.30am–11pm.

Cicala €€€ *Žitná 43, tel: 222 210 375*, www.trattoria.cz. Set in a basement off a busy street that runs east from the top end of Charles Square, Trattoria Cicala serves some of the most authentic, and tastiest, Italian food in the city. The menu offers antipasti, pasta and meat dishes, plus daily specials. Open Mon–Sat noon–3pm and 5.30–10.30pm.

CottoCrudo €€€€€ *Four Seasons Hotel, Veleslavínova 1098/2a, tel: 221 426 880*, www.cottocrudo.cz. Since replacing Allegro (the first Michelin-starred restaurant in post-Communist Eastern Europe) CottoCrudo has lived up to expectations. Set in a wonderful location overlooking the river, not far from the eastern end of the Charles Bridge, chef Luca de Astis offers a delicious array of Italian and Mediterranean dishes. Open daily 7am–12am.

Estella €€ *Opatovická 17, tel: 777 431 344*, www.estrellarestaurant.cz. This excellent vegetarian restaurant serves tasty and inventive dishes, many cooked with organic ingredients. On offer are such classics as vegetarian goulash of seitan or veggie burgers. The Czech wines and beers are worth a try, as are the excellent teas and desserts. Open daily 11.30am–3.30pm and 6–10pm.

Ginger & Fred €€€€€ *Tančící dům, Jiráskovo náměstí 6, tel: 221 984 160*, www.ginger-fred-restaurant.cz. Located on the top floor of one of Prague's most famous modern landmarks, Frank Gehry's 'dancing' or 'Fred and Ginger' building – so called because of its flowing forms – offers sweeping views of the city from both the inside dining room and the rooftop terrace. The menu of international cuisine changes with the seasons. Open daily 11.30am–11pm.

Kolkovna Celnice €€ *V Celnici 1031/4, tel: 224 212 240*, www.kolkovna.cz. Just off náměstí Republiky, this Pilsner Urquell-owned beer hall serves up the usual tasty diet of excellent beer and hearty Bohemian food. This one has the advantage of being on top of one of Prague's best clubs, where you can dance off the dumplings. Open daily 11am–midnight.

Country Life €–€€ *Melantrichova 15, tel: 224 213 366*, www.countrylife. cz. Tucked away in a small street leading south off Old Town Square, this self-service vegetarian eatery is one of the few places in the city that also offers vegan dishes. Non-smoking dining room. Open Mon–Sun 11am–12am.

Flavours Wine&Deli €€€ *Záhřebská 876/29, tel: 725 888 545, www.flavours.cz.* This stylish Vinohrady wine bar is well-known for a wide selection of international as well as Czech and Moravian wines and cheese at reasonable prices. The knowledgeable and friendly staff can recommend wine for the food you're having. They also have a delicatessen. Open Mon–Fri noon–10pm, Sat 2–11pm.

King Solomon €€€€ *Široká 8, tel: 224 818 752, www.kosher.cz.* Fittingly right in the middle of the Jewish Quarter is the only strictly kosher restaurant in Prague with Hebrew-speaking staff. Among the classic dishes of Central European Jewish cooking are chicken soup, gefilte fish, carp with prunes and duckling drumsticks with schollet and sautéed cabbage. Kosher wines are imported from Israel, Hungary and France, as well as offering some from the Czech Republic. It is possible to arrange Shabbat meals beforehand and to have them delivered to your hotel. Open Sun–Thu noon–11pm, Fri dinner by reservation and Sat lunch by reservation only.

Klub Architektů € *Betlémské náměstí 5A, tel: 224 248 878, www.klubarchitektu.com.* Situated just opposite the Bethlehem Church and under an architecture bookshop, this restaurant is a haven of peace. Along with meaty options, there are lots of vegetarian offerings: salads, soups and more exotic dishes, served up in a minimalist, bare-walled cellar. Friendly staff and low prices add to its allure. Open daily 11.30am–midnight.

Kogo €€€€ *Na Příkopě 22, tel: 221 451 259, www.kogo.cz.* A large, bustling, and very popular Mediterranean-style eatery in the contemporary Slovanský Dům arcade on Prague's main shopping street, with a vast range of fish, meat, and pasta dishes. Open daily 11am–11pm.

Kogo Havelská €€€–€€€€ *Havelská 499/27, tel: 224 210 259, http://kogohavelska.cz.* A relaxed but upmarket Italian restaurant and pizzeria located not far from Staroměstské náměstí. It offers the full range of Italian cuisine, with enticing starters and desserts. Breakfast menu also available. Booking is recommended. Open Mon–Fri 8am–11pm, Sat and Sun 10am–11pm.

Kolkovne €€ *V Kolkovně 8, tel: 224 819 701,* www.vkolkovne.cz. Not far from the Spanish Synagogue and on two levels, with gleaming brewery utensils on the ground floor and a cosy basement, this traditional Czech pub offers a contemporary take on Bohemian dishes such as duck and dumplings, accompanied of course by the incomparable brew from Pilsen. The portions are large, hearty and reasonably priced. Open daily 11am–midnight.

Lokal Dlouhááá €€ *Dlouhá 33, tel: 734 283 874,* http://lokal-dlouha. ambi.cz. Set in the heart of the Old Town, this friendly beer hall serves traditional, home-made Czech fare made from fresh ingredients and at reasonable prices. You can also learn how to draw beer form the bartenders, the courses are held in Czech and English. Open Mon–Sat 11am–1am, Sun 11am–midnight.

Mlynec €€€€ *Novotného lávka 9, tel: 227 000 777,* www.mlynec.cz. In a beautiful location by the river, with views of the Charles Bridge. The degustation menu featuring dishes such as *coquilles St-Jacques*, oxtail consommé and saddle of deer is well worth trying. Open daily noon–3pm and 5.30–11pm.

Nostress €€€ *V Kolkovně 907/9, tel: 222 317 007,* www.nostress.cz. Near-by the Spanish Synagogue, this stylish café-restaurant with a contem-porary photography gallery attached is good for its reasonably-priced lunch menu (Kč350). Dinner, however, is much more expensive. The well-executed cooking is generally of the fusion variety. Open Mon–Fri 8.30am–midnight, Sat 10am–midnight, Sun 10am–11pm.

La Veranda €€€€ *Eliśky Krásnohorské 2, Prague 1, tel: 224 814 733,* www. laveranda.cz. A gourmet restaurant near the Spanish Synagogue, La Veranda is a light, stylish venue filled with flowers. It specialises in deli-cate fish dishes but has good meat and vegetarian options too. Cooking styles range from Mediterranean to pan-Asian. Excellent service and above average prices, but certainly worth the splurge. Open Mon–Sat noon–11pm.

Restaurant Ungelt €€€€€ *Týn 638/5, tel: 777 427 000*, www.restaurant-ungelt.cz. In the charming surroundings of the cobbled Týn Court, behind the Týn Church, the Ungelt Restaurant serves primarily fish, but also a variety of meat and vegetarian dishes. The menu is accompanied by an excellent wine list. An outdoor terrace makes a pretty setting for summertime dining. Open daily 11am–midnight.

Universal €€ *V Jirchářích 6, Prague 1, tel: 224 934 416*, www.universal restaurant.cz. About 100 metres (328ft) behind the National Theatre is one of the best-value places in town, serving tasty main courses with a French twist. Meal-sized salads and desserts are as good as you'll find anywhere. A good daily menu at unbelievably reasonable prices. Advance reservations are advisable for peak hours. Open daily 11.30am–11pm.

CASTLE AND LESSER QUARTER

Café Savoy €–€€€ *Vítězná 5, tel: 257 311 562*, http://cafesavoy.ambi.cz. This café in the south corner of the Lesser Quarter, just by the western end of the Legií Bridge, is a good place to stop for refreshment. Choose between excellent French-inspired gourmet food, the café menu or the home-made cakes underneath a beautifully restored neo-Renaissance ceiling. Open Mon–Fri 8am–10.30pm, Sat–Sun 9am–10.30pm.

Coda €€€€ *Tržiště 9, tel: 225 334 761*, www.codarestaurant.cz. Set in the Aria Hotel this smart restaurant has a rooftop terrace offering spectacular views of the Lesser Town and the castle. Beautiful interiors were designed by two Italian architects Rocco Magnoli and Lorenzo Carmellini. It has a good degustation menu of Czech cuisine with traditional *kulajda* soup, roasted duck and plum ravioli, prepared by the Czech chef David Šašek. Open Mon–Sun 7am–11.30pm, live piano Tue–Sat 7.30–10.30pm.

Cukrkavalimonáda €–€€ *Lázeňská 7, tel: 257 225 396*, http://cukrkava limonada.com. On a little square just to the south of Mostecká, 'Sugar-coffee-lemonade' is a beautifully styled café offering variations around scrambled eggs for breakfast, then pastas, frittatas, pancakes and sandwiches throughout the day, and then Mediterranean-style meals in the early evening. Try the home-made pastries and cakes. Open daily 9am–7pm.

Gitanes €€ *Tržiště 7, tel: 257 530 163,* www.gitanes.cz. A quirky and comfortable Bosnian/Serbian/Montenegran restaurant a stone's throw from Malostranské Square. Prettily painted floral ceiling and furnishings, plus a cosy hideaway for two behind a curtain, put you in the right mood. The good Balkan dishes, such as stuffed peppers, home-made lamb sausages and grilled mushrooms, and an eclectic and interesting wine list mean this place is well worth a visit. Open daily 11am–11pm.

Kampa Park €€€€€ *Na Kampě 8b, tel: 257 532 685,* www.kampagroup. com. This well established Czech restaurant is located on Kampa Island near Charles Bridge and is popular not just because of its magnificent setting. Its creative international fare, including mouth-watering fish and seafood are also highly recommended. The extensive wine list features over 150 wines. The riverside terrace is particularly attractive. Open daily 11.30am–1am.

Pálffy Palác €€€€–€€€€€ *Valdštejnská 14, Prague 1, tel: 257 530 522,* www.palffy.cz. Opposite the Waldstein Palace and in operation since the 17th century, this elegant, Baroque restaurant has catered for everyone from diplomats to politicians in its time. An outdoor terrace leads out to breathtaking views of the castle and surrounding gardens. The restaurant's classy continental/French menu features duck breast with preserved oranges, grilled tiger prawns and a selection of fish dishes. Open daily 11am–11pm.

U Malířů 1543 €€€€€ *Maltézské náměstí 11, tel: 257 211 014,* www.umaliru 1543.com. This restaurant is one the most expensive in Prague, found on a quiet square in the Lesser Quarter, just to the east of Karmelitská. French *haute cuisine* is served in a beautiful 16th-century dining room complete with an elaborately decorated ceiling, and a tiny outdoor terrace completes the picture. Absolutely perfect for that special occasion. Open 11.30am–midnight.

U Modré Kachnicky €€€ *Nebovidská 460/6, tel: 257 320 308,* www. umodrekachnicky.cz. 'At the Blue Duckling' is a popular restaurant near Maltézské náměstí, which features Art Nouveau images on the walls and old-fashioned decor, with lots of dark wood and overstuffed chairs. Traditional Czech cuisine is featured on the menu, as is plenty of game and fish. Open daily noon–4pm, 6.30pm–11.30pm.

Olympia €€ *Vítězná 619/7, tel: 251 511 080,* www.kolkovna.cz. Close to the Café Savoy, just by the western end of the Legií Bridge, a restaurant has operated out of this building almost since it opened in 1903. Now, as part of the Pilsner Urquell stable, the emphasis is on comforting Czech butchery, with goose, duck, sausages, pork hocks and lamb knuckles. The cooking is highly creditable and very good value for money. Open daily 11am–midnight.

Terasa U Zlate Studne €€€€€ *U Zlaté studně 166/4, tel: 257 533 322,* www.terasauzlatestudne.cz. Located on the roof of the Golden Well hotel, just a stone's throw from Lesser Town square, this elegant restaurant offers panoramic views of Vltava River and the spires of the Old Town and is ideal for a romantic dinner. The acclaimed chef Pavel Sapic prepares a wonderful range of international dishes. There is a good list of international and Czech wines. Open daily 11am–6pm and 6–11pm.

U Patrona €€€€ *Dražického náměstí 4, Prague 1, tel: 257 530 725,* www. upatrona.cz. These little elegant dining rooms are a good place in which to try well-prepared Bohemian specialities. They include a tasty game *consommé* and excellent roast goose with red cabbage. All helped along by some very smooth service. Open daily 10am–midnight.

A–Z TRAVEL TIPS

A SUMMARY OF PRACTICAL INFORMATION

A

ACCOMMODATION

Prague has many large hotels, but very few old-world, family-run establishments. Most hotels dating from the communist era have very dour exteriors, although many have been renovated, bringing the facilities and interior decoration up to international standards. A few gems from the city's glorious Art Nouveau era have also been refurbished and there are some new luxury 'designer' hotels.

While Prague is popular all year round, it becomes very crowded with visitors from June to September and around Christmas, when booking a few weeks ahead is essential.

Hotel prices often appear in euros. Always ask whether the room rate includes tax before you make a firm booking as this can add 21 percent or more to the bill.

If you arrive in the city without accommodation, contact the Prague City Tourism (tel: 12 444; www.prague.eu).

I'd like a single room/ double room. **Chtěl bych jednolůžkový pokoj/dvoulůžkový pokoj.**
with bath/with shower **s koupelnou/se sprchou**
What's the rate per day? **Kolik stojí za den?**

B&Bs. The number of private homes offering bed-and-breakfast accommodation has grown dramatically in recent years. Listings can be found at www.praguewelcome.cz or www.czech-homestays.com.

AIRPORT

Václav Havel Airport Prague (www.prg.aero/en/) is situated 10km (6.5 miles) northwest of the city. Airport express bus operated by the public transport authority (www.dpp.cz/en) runs between the airport and the main railway station in the city centre every 15–30 minutes from 5am–10.30pm. The journey takes about 30 minutes to Hlavní Nádraži (Kč60). Tickets may be purchased from the bus driver. A cheaper (Kč32) but lengthier option is the No. 119 bus, which travels to the metro line A and the No. 100 and 179 buses to the metro line B. Buy tickets in the terminal or from the machine at the bus stop. The reliable AAA radiotaxi firm (tel: 14 014 or 222 333 222; www.aaataxi. cz) has a rank just outside the arrivals hall and the trip to the centre should not cost more than Kč650.

B

BICYCLE RENTAL

While some parts of Prague are quite hilly (and therefore hard work), hiring a bike to get around, especially along the river, can be good fun and convenient. To hire a modern off-road bike with gears and a light-weight aluminium frame, contact **Praha Bike** (tel: 732 388 880; www. prahabike.cz). A day's hire costs Kč590.

BUDGETING FOR YOUR TRIP

Due to the strength of the Czech *koruna* Prague is no longer a particularly cheap destination for visitors from the UK.

Hotel: Mid-range hotel per room per night Kč4,000–5,000.

Meals and drinks: Large glass of beer Kč30–40 (as much as Kč90 in touristy establishments such as those on Old Town Square); three-course dinner per person Kč350–650; soft drink Kč35.

Entertainment: Theatre tickets Kč400–1,000 with state company, or international performances from around Kč1,200. Concert tickets are Kč100–500.

Tours: City walking tour (3 hours) Kč350; coach tour to Karlštejn Castle (5 hours) around Kč1,000.

Prague Tourist Card: Kč1550 for two days, Kč1810 for three days and Kč2080 for five days. The card includes entry to more than 50 sights and museums, unlimited use of public transport, a coach tour of Prague, a shuttle bus to the airport, a cruise on the Vltava River and a guided walking tour. It can be purchased at the airport, tourist information centres or at www.praguecard.com.

C

CAMPING

A large campsite on the banks of the Vltava, **Autocamp Trojská** (Trojská 375/157, Prague 7; tel: 283 850 487; www.autocamp-trojska.cz; open all year) not far from Troja Palace and the zoo, is the closest to the town centre. It has space for caravans and tents with good, if not luxurious, facilities. The Prague Information Service (tel: 12 444; www.prague.eu) has details of other campsites.

CAR HIRE

If you plan to stay in the city rather than touring the countryside, a car may be less of a help than a hindrance. If you do want to hire a vehicle, most of the major international firms operate in Prague.

Drivers must be at least 21 years of age and have held a full driving licence for one year. The daily hire charge for a medium-sized car (by European standards) is around Kč2,000–3,500 per day with unlimited mileage. Most companies will have special rates for weekends.

Pricing structures can be complicated and extras can include local tax (21 percent), additional driver charge, mileage, airport delivery charge and collision-damage waiver. Collision-damage waiver is not compulsory but limits your liability in case of an accident. It adds around Kč230 per day to the rental cost.

Avis: airport, tel: 235 362 420; Klimentská 46, Prague 1, tel: 221 851 225; www.avis.cz.

A-Rent Car: V Celnici 8 (Millennium Plaza), Prague 1, tel: 602 489 394; www.arentcar.cz.

I'd like to rent a car. **Chtěl bych si půjčit auto.**
large/small **velké/malé**
for one day/a week **na jeden den/týden**
Please include full insurance. **Prosím, započítejte plné pojištění.**

Hertz: airport, tel: 225 345 021; Evropska15, Prague 6, tel: 225 345 041, www.hertz.cz.
Europcar: airport, tel: 235 364 531; Elišky Krásnohorské 9, Prague 1, tel: 232 000 600; www.europcar.cz.
Sixt: reservation, tel: 222 324 995; www.sixt.cz.

CLIMATE

Prague tends to experience continental weather patterns springing from Russia, but also mild, wet weather from the Atlantic. Winters are on the whole cold and wet, but it can stay dry and clear for long spells. When the wind blows from Russia, it can be extremely cold. Summers are warm but rainy. June and July are two of the rainiest months of the year, while spring and autumn are changeable.

		J	F	M	A	M	J	J	A	S	O	N	D
Max	**°F**	50	52	64	73	82	88	91	90	84	71	57	50
	°C	10	11	18	23	28	31	33	32	29	22	14	10
Min	**°F**	9	10	18	28	36	45	48	46	39	28	23	14
	°C	-13	-12	-8	-2	2	7	9	8	4	-2	-5	-10

CLOTHING

Practical, casual clothing suits most occasions. In summer, bring light-weight clothing but be prepared for showers, and a warm layer in case it's cool in the evenings. In spring and autumn, a coat or thick jacket is advisable. In winter, take a coat, hat and gloves. For the opera or ballet, or dinner in a fine restaurant, smart clothing is appropriate.

CRIME AND SAFETY

Prague is a safe, pleasant city to explore on foot. Violent crime is rare, although petty crime has risen in parallel with the growing number of visitors. Stay alert on trams (especially No. 22) and the metro, and in large crowds, for example on Charles Bridge or in Wenceslas Square, where pickpockets might be at work. Stick to well-lit streets at night.

> I want to report a theft. **Chci ohlásit krádež.**
> My wallet/handbag/passport/ ticket has been stolen.
> **Ukradli mi náprsní tašku peněženku/kabelku/pas/ lístek.**

D

DRIVING

Road conditions. Road conditions in the Czech Republic are generally good, although signs are not always clear so you will need a good map. Prague it-self suffers from severe congestion. Drivers are generally patient, but keep a lookout out for trams, as well as cobbled streets and tramlines, both of which become slippery when wet, and also for confusing one-way systems.

Rules and regulations. Drive on the right and overtake on the left. The speed limits are 130 kmh (80 mph) on motorways, 90 kmh (56 mph) on secondary roads and 50 kmh (31 mph) in built-up areas.

Seat belts are compulsory where fitted, and drink-driving is illegal. Headlights must be kept on at all times in winter. Children under the age of 12 are not allowed in the front seat.

Parking. Parking in the city poses some difficulties (try by the railway station on Wilsonova). On-street parking is divided into zones: orange for short-term parking at Kč80 per hour; green for stays of up to 6 hours, at Kč60 per hour; purple unlimited for residents or permit holders and for others for maximum 24 hours at Kč40 per hour. Chargeable parking hours are generally Mon–Fri 8am–8pm. It is not regulated outside these hours so it is possible to park your car free of charge then.

If you need help. Dial 1240 to call out Autoklub Bohemia Assistance, who will attempt to repair your car or take you to the nearest garage. Call 158 for the police.

Jednosměrný provoz One way
Na silnice se pracuje Roadworks
Nebezpeči Danger
Nevstupujte No entry
Objížďka Diversion
Opatrně/Pozor Caution
Pěší zóna Pedestrian zone
Snížit rychlost (zpomalit) Slow down
Vchod Entrance
Východ Exit

Full tank, please. **Plnou nádrž, prosím.**
super/unleaded/diesel **super/bezolovnatý/nafta**
I've broken down. **Mám poruchu.**
There's been an accident. **Stala se nehoda.**
Can I park here? **Mohu zde parkovat?**

E

ELECTRICITY

Prague uses the 220V/50 Hz AC current, requiring standard two-pin round European plugs. Visitors should bring their own adapters.

EMBASSIES AND CONSULATES

Ireland: Tržiště 13, Prague 1; tel: 257 011 280; www.dfa.ie/irish-embas sy/czech-republic.

UK: Thunovská 14, Prague 1; tel: 257 402 111; www.gov.uk/world/organ isations/british-embassy-prague.

EMERGENCIES

General Emergencies: 112; **Police:** 158; **Fire Brigade:** 150; **Ambu-lance:** 155.

Fire! **Hoří!**
Help! **Pomoc!**
Stop thief! **Chyťte zloděje!**

G

GETTING THERE

By air. The national airline is ČSA (České Aeroline; www.csa.cz); they and British Airways (www.britishairways.com) fly direct to Prague from London. Numerous budget airlines now fly to the city and from the UK these include: easyJet, from Gatwick, Bristol, Edinburgh, Manchester and Stansted (www.easyjet.com); Ryanair from Edinburgh, Liverpool and Stansted (www.ryanair.com) Wizzair from Luton (www.wizzair.com) and Jet2 from Belfast, Birmingham, East Midlands, Glasgow, Leeds-Bradford, Manchester, and Newcastle (www.jet2.com). The Czech-based Smart Wings flies from elsewhere in Europe (www.smartwings.com).

By rail. Prices for rail travel are often more expensive than air travel and the journeys take longer. Purchasing a rail pass for a set amount of days can help minimise costs. Tickets can be purchased at railway sta-tion or from Czech Railways (České dráhy; tel: 221 111 122; www.cd.cz).

The most direct way to reach Prague from London by train is via Paris and Frankfurt, which takes around 18 hours (for information and bookings, visit www.voyages-sncf.com). Most of the international trains arrive at the main station Praha hlavní nádraží, also known as Wilson Station, but some of them call at Smíchov.

By road. Eurolines (www.eurolines.com) operates buses that connect the major cities of Europe. To bring your own car you will need a valid driving licence; vehicle registration/ownership documents; a Green Card; a national identity sticker; a first-aid kit; and a red warning triangle. To drive on motorways and dual carriageways, a windscreen sticker (a *vignette*, Kč440 for a month and Kč310 for ten days), available at the border, post offices and at filling stations, must be displayed.

GUIDES AND TOURS

A number of tours are available in Prague and into the surrounding countryside. These include walking tours (individual and group), themed tours, a trip on a historic tram or by boat down the Vltava, lasting anything from 30 minutes to a whole day. Some tours home in on specific themes – the history of the Jewish community, Romanesque Prague, Gothic Prague, Baroque Prague, Renaissance Prague or Composers' Prague.

Registered English-speaking guides can be hired by the hour by individuals or groups. Contact the Prague Information Service for more information (see page 131).

H

HEALTH AND MEDICAL CARE

Citizens of EU countries including the UK are entitled to free emergency treatment in the Czech Republic. Make sure you have your European Health Insurance Card before travelling. You will be charged for any further treatment, so it still makes sense to take out adequate health and accident insurance.

A number of medical facilities with English-speaking medical personnel cater specifically to visitors. There are several foreign clinics in Prague:

Canadian Medical Care (www.cmcpraha.cz), EUC Premium (www.eucpremium.cz) or Unicare Medical Center (www.unicare.cz). The Foreigner's department of the **Hospital Na Homolce** is located at Roentgenova 2, Prague 5, tel: 257 273 289, www.homolka.cz. For first aid visit **Health Center Prague** at Vodičkova 28–30, Prague 2, tel: 224 220 040, www.doctor-prague.cz.

Pharmacies. For minor health problems visit a pharmacy – look for a green cross, or the word *lékárna* on the front of the shop. There are 24-hour facilities at Belgická 37 (tel: 224 946 982) and Palackého 5 (tel: 224 946 982). Though the range of drugs available is not as wide as in Western Europe or the US, you will still be able to find remedies for most minor illnesses.

L

LANGUAGE

The national language is Czech. However, English is widely spoken, as is German. If you can learn and use a few Czech words, it will always be appreciated. The Czech alphabet has 33 letters; for instance, c and č are counted as two different letters. Here are a few tips on the pronunciation of the more difficult sounds:

ch like English **h**
ě like **ye** in *yes*
ň like the **n** in Ca*n*ute
ř like **rs** in Pe*rs*ian
j like **y** in *y*ellow

Do you speak English? **Mluvíte anglicky?**
I don't speak Czech. **Nemluvím česky.**
Good morning/Good afternoon **Dobré jitro/Dobré odpoledne**
Good evening/Good night **Dobrý večer/Dobrou noc**
Please/Thank you **Prosím/Děkuji Vám**
That's all right/You're welcome. **To je v pořádku.**

š like the **sh** in s*h*ine
č like **ch** in *ch*urch
c like **ts** in *ts*etse
ž like the **s** in plea*s*ure

LGBTQ TRAVELLERS

Gay and lesbian travellers will generally find Prague an easy-going destination, though very overt displays of affection might attract stares. The gay scene is small. For up-to-date information, see www.prague. gayguide.net; the main lesbian website (all in Czech) is www.lesba.cz.

M

MAPS

Free maps are available from the Prague Information Service (www. prague.eu) and some hotels.

MEDIA

Newspapers. The English-language online newspaper, the *Prague Post* (www.praguepost.com) contains news and comment as well as events listings. The Czech News Agency (www.ceskenoviny.cz) also provides news in English. Another good resource is *Prague in Your Pocket* (www. inyourpocket.com) with events and entertainment listings.

TV. Satellite television has one or more English-speaking news channels. The main ones are CNN and BBC World.

Radio. Radio Praha broadcasts news in English from Mon to Fri at 8pm on 92.6 FM; www.radio.cz.

MONEY

The currency of the Czech Republic is the crown or *koruna* (Kč). Each crown is theoretically made up of 100 hellers (hal.), but they are not used. There are 5,000 Kč, 2,000 Kč, 1,000 Kč, 500 Kč, 200 Kč and 100 Kč notes; and coins of 20 Kč, 10 Kč, 5 Kč, 2 Kč and 1 Kč.

Currency exchange. Banks open 8am–5pm, some close at lunch time. Most charge a standard 1 percent commission. Bureaux de change often open until 10pm, but they are best avoided as they can charge up to 30 percent commission. There are a large number of ATMs that will issue cash against your current-account card or credit card; this is generally the easiest way to get money.

Credit cards. Credit cards are increasingly accepted for payment across the city. This includes most hotels, but it is still wise to check.

O

OPENING TIMES

Banks are open 8am–5pm (some close from noon–1pm) Monday to Friday. Bureaux de change operate daily, often until 10pm or later.

Some general shops open as early as 6am, while department stores open at 8.30am; both close at around 6pm, although a growing number stay open till 8pm on Thursday. Shops in the centre, particularly those aimed at tourists, often remain open until late in summer.

Museums usually open 10am–6pm and close on Sunday or Monday; exceptions include the Jewish Museum's synagogues (closed Saturday). Most galleries open 10am–6pm but close on Monday.

P

POLICE

There are several types of police operating in the city. **State police** (tel: 158; www.policie.cz) are responsible for day-to-day policing. They wear white shirts and dark-grey trousers or skirts. They are armed. The best police station to contact is the one in Můstek, at Jungmannovo náměstí 9, Prague 1 (tel: 974 851 750), because there are always interpreters of several languages. **Municipal police** (tel: 156; www.mppraha.cz) wear light-grey trousers or skirts. **Traffic police** are responsible for all road and traffic regulations. They may erect roadblocks to check documents (always carry your driving licence, passport and your car documents) or to breathalyse drivers. This police force also controls fines for parking and clamping infringements.

POST OFFICES

Postal services (www.ceskaposta.cz) are cheap and reliable for letters and postcards. Most shops that sell postcards also sell stamps, as do many hotels. Postboxes are either orange with a side slit or orange-and-blue with a front flap. The main post office (open 24 hours) is at Jindřišská 909/14, just off Wenceslas Square. Here you can make international calls, and buy stamps and phonecards. Local post offices generally open Mon–Fri 8am–7pm. Postal rates at the time of printing were: Europe from Kč32.

PUBLIC HOLIDAYS

Government offices and banks close for the following holidays:

1 January *Nový rok* New Year's Day

1 May *Svátek práce* May Day

8 May *Vítězství nad fašismem* Victory over fascism

5 July *Slovanští věrozvěsti sv. Cyril a Metoděj* Slavic Missionaries St Cyril and St Methodius

6 July *Výročí úmrtí Jana Husa* Jan Hus's death

28 September *Den české státnosti* Day of the Czech Statehood

28 October *První československá republika* First Czechoslovak Republic

17 November *Den boje za svobodu a demokracii* Day of Struggle for Liberty and Democracy

24 December *Štědrý den* Christmas Eve

25/26 December *Svátek vánoční* Christmas/Boxing Day

Movable date *Velikonoční pondělí* Easter Monday

R

RELIGION

The Czech Republic is not conspicuously religious but is a mainly

Catholic country. Prague has a profusion of churches that hold regular services and some also hold services in English. Times will be posted outside the church, or consult the *Prague Post* (www.praguepost.com). Within the city there is an active Jewish community. There are also Anglican and Baptist churches.

T

TELEPHONES

Most phone numbers consist of nine digits, including the area code. You should dial the entire nine-digit number even if you are dialling within the same area code. Public telephones take phonecards *(telefonní karta)*. These can be bought at post offices or newsstands.

The international code for the Czech Republic is 420. The city code for Prague is 2, but this is included in the nine-digit number.

To make an international call dial 00, then the country code, then the number.

For Prague directory enquiries call 1180. The international operator can be contacted on 1181.

Most international mobile phones will work in Prague. However, for longer stays it is better and much cheaper to buy one of the easily available local pay-as-you-go SIM cards. The main companies are O2 (www.cz.o2.com), T-Mobile (www.t-mobile.cz) and Vodafone (www.vodafone.cz).

TIME ZONES

Prague operates on Central European Time (CET). This is one hour ahead of GMT in winter and two hours ahead of GMT in summer.

TIPPING

Tipping is appreciated but levels are low (it is enough to round up the bill, or to leave the change) and in some restaurants, service is included in the price; it should state this on the menu.

TOILETS

There are public toilets at each metro station and shopping centre. There is usually a small fee of around 5–10 Kč.

If there are no man or woman symbols to help you, ladies' toilets will be labelled *Ženy* or *Dámy*, mens' will be *Muži* or *Páni*.

TOURIST INFORMATION

For information before you leave for Prague contact the Czech Tourist Authority (www.czechtourism.com), at the following:

UK: Prudence Place, Proctor Way, Luton LU2 9PE, tel: 1582 725874; email: london@czechtourism.com.

US: 1109 Madison Avenue, New York, NY 10028, tel: 212 288 0830; email: newyork@czechtourism.com.

The **Czech Tourist Authority**'s information centre in Prague is at Vinohradska 46. **Prague City Tourism** (www.prague.eu). Information centres can be found at the Old Town Hall, Staroměstské náměstí 1, Prague 1, Rytířska 31, Prague 1, and Wenceslas Square, Prague 1. There are also many commercial agencies offering tourist information and selling tours.

TRANSPORT

Prague has a comprehensive and well-integrated public-transport system (www.dpp.cz) that provides a cheap and efficient service. Tickets and passes can be used on all forms of transport. Each ticket has a time limit and you pay more for a longer limit. The cheapest ticket costs Kč24 and allows either 30 minutes of travel with no transfer or five stops on the metro with no line change. A Kč32 ticket allows 90 minutes of travel and allows line change or tram transfer within that time. Children aged six to 15 pay half price; children under six and people over 70 travel free of charge.

Tickets can be bought at metro stations (there are automatic ticket machines which give instructions in English and supply change) or newsstands and some shops. They must be validated in the small yellow machines before you catch the tram or arrive at the metro.

Day tickets or longer passes are also available and are valid for unlimited travel on all forms of transport. They are valid from the date stamped on them and do not have to be validated for each journey. Prices are as follows: 24-hour pass Kč110; three-day pass Kč310. The Prague Tourist Card (see page 119) also includes free travel on public transport.

Buses and Trams. Buses, which are clean and punctual, tend to provide a service out to the Prague suburbs rather than compete with trams in the city. There is a comprehensive network of tram routes which connect both sides of the river. Each tram stop shows the tram number passing there and a timetable. Most city maps show the tram routes in addition to the location of the major attractions. All trams run from 4.30am–midnight, but a number of routes are also designated as night routes and operate a service 24 hours a day. Purchase your ticket before you travel and validate it as you enter, unless you are transferring from another tram or metro within your allotted time.

Metro. The extremely efficient Prague metro opened in 1974 and provides a great service for visitors. There are three interlinked lines, and metro maps can be found at each station. Metro signs above ground feature a stylised M incorporated into an arrow pointing downwards. The metro operates from around 5am–midnight.

Funicular at Petřín. The ride to the top of Petřín Hill also takes standard tickets. You can buy these at the station before you travel.

Taxis. The most common complaint from visitors to Prague tends to be about taxis; there are some unscrupulous operators out there. Prices are supposed to be about Kč40 then Kč28 per km, with an additional charge of Kč6 per minute for waiting. Phoning a taxi is cheaper than hailing one, as

Where do I get the bus to the city centre/airport? **Odkud jede autobus do centra města?/na letiště?**
Take these bags to the bus/taxi, please. **Prosím, odneste tato zavazadla k autobusu/taxi.**

rates are lower and you won't be overcharged. Two reputable firms with staff who speak English are aaa Taxi (tel: 222 333 222; www.aaataxi.cz) and Profi Taxi (tel: 140 15; www.profitaxi.cz). If you must hail a taxi, check the rates listed on the passenger door with the meter, or negotiate a price.

V

VISAS AND ENTRY REQUIREMENTS

Passports/visas. Citizens of the EU need only a passport to visit the Czech Republic for up to 180 days.

Customs. It is illegal to export antiques without a permit.

W

WEBSITES AND INTERNET ACCESS

A few websites that may help in the planning of your trip:

www.czechtourism.com Czech Tourist Authority

www.prague.eu Prague Information Service

www.praha.eu The official Prague tourism website.

www.czechspecials.cz All you need to know about Czech cuisine

There are a number of internet cafés in Prague, including: Bohemia Bagel (Masná 2, Prague 1; tel: 224 812 560; www.bohemiabagel.cz) and The Globe Bookstore (Pštrossova 6, Prague 1; tel: 224 934 203; www.globebookstore.cz).

Y

YOUTH HOSTELS

The website of the national youth hostel association (www.czech hostels.com) has details of all the official hostels.

Miss Sophie's Hostel, Melounova 3, Prague 2; tel: 246 032 620; www.miss-sophies.com.

Travellers' Hostel, Dlouhá 33, Prague 1; tel: 777 738 608; www.travellers.cz.

RECOMMENDED HOTELS

Prague has long been one of Europe's most popular tourist destinations. The shortage of accommodation which marked the immediate post-communist years is a thing of the past; new hotels are constantly being added to the city's stock, the majority of them at the upper end of the scale. Some are of outstanding quality, located in historic buildings or featuring the best that contemporary designers have to offer.

Accommodation is relatively expensive and good budget accommodation – such as small, family-owned hotels – is lacking. However, the situation is improving. It is always best to reserve your room well in advance, especially from June–September and at Christmas time, this way you can get better prices and special offers. Rates given below are for the cheapest double room per night in high season and may be listed in euros. Room taxes of 21 percent and a small municipal tax may be extra, so check before booking. Breakfast is not always included. Disabled access is generally better in the more modern hotels.

The following hotel recommendations – price categories indicated in euro symbols – cover all areas of the city, including large and small hotels with local and international management.

If telephoning Prague from outside the Czech Republic dial 00+420 before the numbers listed.

€€€€€	over Kč6,000
€€€€	Kč5,000–6,000
€€€	Kč4,000–5,000
€€	Kč3,000–4,000
€	below Kč3000

OLD TOWN AND NEW TOWN

987 Prague €€€€€ *Senovázné náměstí 15/987, Prague 1, tel: 255 737 200*, www.987praguehotel.com. In the north of the New Town is this über-chic design hotel. With Phillip Starck fixtures and Aera Saarinena and Arne Jacobsen furniture, it epitomises a certain kind of northern European cool design. Great if you like it, but this is not the cheapest place in town.

Adria €€€ *Václavské náměstí (Wenceslas Square) 26, Prague 1, tel: 221 081 111,* www.hoteladria.cz. This bright, yellow-hued hotel in an enviable position on Wenceslas Square features 89 rooms with polished wood furniture and green-and-gold fixtures. You can book theatre tickets and sightseeing tours at the front desk. All rooms here have internet access, room service and satellite television. Several rooms are suitable for guests with disabilities.

Four Seasons €€€€€ *Veleslavínova 2a/1098, Prague 1, tel: 221 427 000,* www.fourseasons.com/prague. Everything you would expect from this well respected hotel chain, this 157-room hotel on the bank of the River Vltava offers stunning views. All rooms have luxury down pillows and duvets, mini-bar, high-speed internet access and CD players. Spa and fitness centre. Restaurant, bar and 24 hour in-room dining.

Grand Hotel Praha €€ *Staroměstské náměstí 481/22, Prague 1, tel: 221 632 556,* www.grandhotelpraha.cz. This beautiful hotel occupies three historical buildings on the Old Town Square. Rooms have wooden beams and period furniture, along with internet access, satellite TV and air conditioning. It may be a little on the noisy side, but it has a great view of the Astronomical Clock, especially from the baroque Café Mozart on the first floor.

Hotel Josef €€€€ *Rybná 20, Prague 1, tel: 221 700 111,* www.hoteljosef. com. A sleek designer hotel near the Jewish Quarter. The interior, designed by Eva Jiricna, has stone-and-glass bathrooms attached to minimalist rooms. None of this is cheap (up to around Kč7,000), but it does make a change from the often heritage-heavy accommodation available elsewhere in the city.

Maximilian €€€€ *Haštalská 14, Prague 1, tel: 225 303 111,* www.maxi milianhotel.com. This hotel close to the Jewish Quarter and St Agnes's

Convent is a bargain for both its position and the clean lines of the modern rooms. The rooms have nice little designer touches and comfortable beds, some have good views over the Old Town. As an added bonus the hotel contains the Planet Zen Wellness Studio.

Mosaic House € Odborů 4, *Prague 2, tel: 221 595 350*, www.mosaichouse. com. This beautifully designed hostel has 42 shared and 55 private rooms, all with private bathrooms; the top-floor ones have terraces with views of the city. The hostel provides the facilities of a four-star hotel. Guests are invited to party at the La Loca Music Bar and Lounge.

Museum Pension € *Mezibranská 15, Prague 1, tel: 296 325 186*, www. hotelmuseum.cz. A fantastic pension in a very central location next to the National Museum. Rooms are very large and all face a quiet garden courtyard. Excellent value for money and perfect for families. Great buffet breakfasts.

Palace Praha €€€€€ *Panská 12, Prague 1, tel: 224 093 111*, www.palace hotel.cz. Just a quick walk from Wenceslas Square, the Art Nouveau Palace Hotel is arguably one of the most luxurious and elegant hotels in the city. With its extravagant Art Nouveau décor and bathrooms lined with Carrara marble, each room provides a long list of amenities to impress the discerning traveller, including air conditioning, mini-bar, and internet connection. Its sister hotel, the Art Deco Imperial Hotel (www. hotel-imperial.cz), will appeal to lovers of the later art form.

Paris €€€€ *U Obecního domu 1, Prague 1, tel: 222 195 195*, www.hotel-paris.cz. The Hotel Paris, situated next to the Municipal House, was one of Prague's finest establishments when it was built in 1904. Today it has been totally refurbished and is once again at its dazzling best. If you don't stay here, at least visit the Café de Paris for a drink. Facilities include gourmet restaurant, fitness room, Brandeis Clinic (aesthetic medicine), 24-hour room service. 86 rooms.

Grandium €€€€€ *Politických vězňů 913/12, Prague 1, tel: 234 100 100*, www.hotel-grandium.cz. In a street running parallel to Wenceslas Square, this stunning designer establishment is linked to Prague's most famous thoroughfare by an arcade. Its 197 luxurious rooms and suites in shades of green and grey are fully equipped. There is a bar, a noodle restaurant and an interior garden.

CASTLE DISTRICT AND LESSER QUARTER

Aria €€€€ *Tržiště 9, Prague 1, tel: 225 334 111,* www.ariahotel.net. In the same street as the US embassy, this addition to Prague's growing array of accommodation is distinguished by its musical theme and by the sumptuousness and design quality of bedrooms and public spaces. Some rooms overlook the baroque Vrtba garden and there's a stunning rooftop restaurant.

Design Hotel Neruda €€€€ *Nerudova 44, Prague 1, tel: 257 535 557,* www.designhotelneruda.com. A stone's throw from the castle, this 1348 building now has a minimalist modern interior. The rates reflect its location, but the rooms are clean and comfortable, and there is a pleasant café space with good coffee and hot chocolate, overlooking the busy climb up to the castle.

Domus Balthazar €€–€€€ *Mostecká 5, Prague 1, tel: 257 199 499,* www. domus-balthasar.cz. A design hotel in the heart of Malá Strana with modern furniture complementing the old beams of the rooms. It is in a quite busy location but the hotel is very convenient for most of the sights in the centre of town and the rates are fairly reasonable. It has a sister hotel, Domus Henrici (www.domus-henrici.cz/) near Prague Castle.

Dům u tří čápů €€€€ *Valdštejnské náměstí 20/8, Prague 1, tel: 257 210 779,* www.hotelthreestorks.cz. This design hotel close to the Waldstein Palace is excellent. Very chic, all clean lines and modern furniture, but without disturbing the original fabric of this historic building. The rooms are not only beautifully done but also very central and quiet, and the restaurant is also recommended.

Dům u velké boty €€–€€€ *Vlašská 30/333, Prague 1, tel: 257 532 088,* www.dumuvelkeboty.cz. This small B&B is in a superb location. The building dates from the early 17th century, and care has been taken to ensure that the interior and furniture maintain the historic feel. Lovely comfy beds, spotless bathrooms and friendly owners all go towards making this one of the best places to stay in the city. Cash only.

Hoffmeister €€€€€ *Pod Bruskou 7, Prague 1, tel: 251 017 111,* www. hoffmeister.cz. This family-owned hotel is situated near the foot of the Old Castle steps and is less than five minutes' walk from Malostranská metro station. Each room is individually and well furnished with original art by Adolf Hoffmeister, father of the present owner. Rooms have air conditioning, TV, Wi-Fi, phone and mini-bar. Facilities include an on-site spa, a gourmet restaurant and a café with a pretty terrace.

Mandarin Oriental €€€€€ *Nebovidská 459/1, Prague 1, tel: 233 088 888,* www.mandarinoriental.com/prague. This impeccable establishment in one of the most tranquil parts of the Lesser Quarter has been carefully inserted into the historic fabric of a medieval monastery. Faultless service and a range of facilities including a unique spa set in a restored chapel.

Savoy €€€€ *Keplerova 218/6, Prague 1, tel: 224 302 430,* www.hotel savoyprague.com. An elegant Art Nouveau hotel overlooking the spires of the castle district. Rooms are decorated in lush red, bathrooms in marble and chrome. Amenities include 24-hour room service, a hair salon and a restaurant serving Czech and international cuisine.

U Krále Karla €€–€€€€ *Úvoz 4/170, Prague 1, tel: 257 531 211,* www. ukralekarla.cz. This baroque building (it took its present form in 1639) is in a quiet and convenient location at the top of the hill, looking out over Petřín Hill. The big rooms have rustic decor with vaulted or painted wood ceilings. Facilities include a restaurant and lobby bar, and free parking.

FURTHER AFIELD

Hotel Absolutum €€€ *Jablonského 4, Prague 7, tel: 222 541 406,* www.ab solutumhotel.cz. This modern, somewhat business-like hotel is a good place to stay if you are looking for a bit of luxury at a reasonable price.

The rooms are nicely done (as are the bathrooms) and spacious. The Salut restaurant is a good place for lunch.

Andel's €€€ *Stroupežnického 21, Prague 5, tel: 296 889 688*, www.vi-hotels.com. All sharp angles, glass and rough stone, Andel's is flanked by a shopping mall and various eateries. Rooms are designed in minimalist style with glass desks, concealed lighting, Wi-Fi and DVD players. There is also a restaurant, health club and conference centre. The historic centre is a short tram ride or two Metro stops away.

Angelo €€€ *Radlická 3216/1g, Prague 5, tel: 234 801 111*, www.vi-hotels.com. With its cheerful Jazz Bar, this designer hotel is a good place to stay outside of the city centre. The rooms are nicely done in black, red and yellow. The building is perhaps better looking on the outside than from the rather corporate corridors, but for a business hotel it is pretty decent.

Pension 15 € *Vlkova 15, Prague 3, tel: 222 719 768*, www.pension15.cz. Spotless, if slightly spartan rooms with shared bathrooms and apartments at very good prices. Well-run and modern, this is an excellent budget option not far from the tram stops on Seifertova. Breakfast and parking for additional charge. Cash only.

INDEX

INSIGHT ⊙ GUIDES POCKET GUIDE

PRAGUE

First Edition 2018

Editor: Rachel Lawrence
Author: Lindsay Bennett
Head of Production: Rebeka Davies
Picture Editor: Tom Smyth
Cartography Update: Carte
Update Production: Apa Digital
Photography Credits: 123RF 66, 68, 80,
83; Apa Publications 5TC; 5M, 17, 64, 104;
Bigstock 86; Getty Images 4MC, 15, 22, 24,
29, 58, 72; iStock 4TC, 4TL, 5MC, 5M, 11, 13,
18, 21, 26, 34, 41, 45, 46, 48, 50, 52, 55, 63,
84, 90, 97, 98, 102, 105; iStock 1, 5MC, 6L, 7,
36, 57; Národní divadlo 5T; Public domain 89;
Rod Purcell/Apa Publications 35, 38, 39, 43,
49, 61, 71, 75, 77, 79, 91, 92, 93, 94, 101, 103;
Shutterstock 4ML, 6R, 7R, 33, 65, 106
Cover Picture: Shutterstock

Distribution
UK, Ireland and Europe: Apa Publications
(UK) Ltd; sales@insightguides.com
United States and Canada: Ingram
Publisher Services; ips@ingramcontent.com
Australia and New Zealand: Woodslane;
info@woodslane.com.au
Southeast Asia: Apa Publications (SN) Pte;
singaporeoffice@insightguides.com
Worldwide: Apa Publications (UK) Ltd;
  sales@insightguides.com

**Special Sales, Content Licensing
and CoPublishing**
Insight Guides can be purchased in bulk
quantities at discounted prices. We can
create special editions, personalised jackets
and corporate imprints tailored to your
needs. sales@insightguides.biz;
www.insightguides.biz

All Rights Reserved
© 2018 Apa Digital (CH) AG and
Apa Publications (UK) Ltd

Printed in China by CTPS

No part of this book may be reproduced,
stored in a retrieval system or transmitted in
any form or means mechanical, mechanical,
photocopying, recording or otherwise,
without prior written permission from Apa
Publications.

Contact us
Every effort has been made to provide
accurate information in this publication,
but changes are inevitable. The publisher
cannot be responsible for any resulting loss,
inconvenience or injury. We would appreciate
it if readers would call our attention to any
errors or outdated information. We also
welcome your suggestions; please contact
us at: hello@insightguides.com
www.insightguides.com

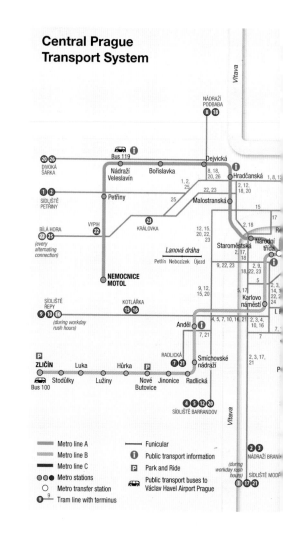

Central Prague
Transport System

Vltava

NÁDRAŽÍ
PODBABA
8 18

Bus 119

DIVOKÁ
ŠÁRKA
20 26

Nádraží
Veleslavín

Bořislavka

Dejvická

8, 18,
20, 26

Hradčanská   1, 8, 12

SÍDLIŠTĚ
PETŘINY
1 2

Petřiny

1, 2,
25

22, 23

25

2, 12,
18, 20

Malostranská

15

17

BÍLÁ HORA
23 25
(every
alternating
connection)

VYPICH
22

KRÁLOVKA
23

12, 15,
20, 22,
23

Lanová dráha
Petřín Nebozizek Újezd

2, 18

Staroměstská

2, 17,
18

Národní
třída

Re

NEMOCNICE
MOTOL

9, 22, 23

2, 9,
18, 22, 23

5

SÍDLIŠTĚ
ŘEPY
9 10 16
(during workday
rush hours)

KOTLÁŘKA
15 16

Andělo
7, 21

9, 12,
15, 20

5, 17

Karlovo
náměstí

4, 5, 7, 10, 16, 21

2, 3, 4,
10, 16

2, 3,
14, 17,
22, 24

I. P

7,

7

ZLIČÍN

Luka

Hůrka

Stodůlky

Lužiny

Nové
Butovice

Jinonice

Radlická

RADLICKÁ
7 21

Smíchovské
nádraží

2, 3, 17,
21

P

Bus 100

SÍDLIŠTĚ BARRANDOV
4 5 12 20

Vltava

2 3
NÁDRAŽÍ BRANÍ

(during
workday rush
hours)

SÍDLIŠTĚ MODŘ
9 17 21

▬▬ Metro line A	▬ Funicular
▬▬ Metro line B	❶ Public transport information
▬▬ Metro line C	🅿 Park and Ride
●●● Metro stations	🚌 Public transport buses to
○ Metro transfer station	Václav Havel Airport Prague
❾ ⁹ Tram line with terminus	

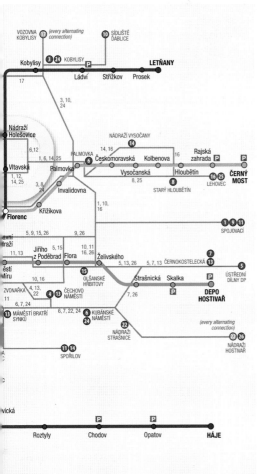